Miniatures and Moods

MINIATURES
AND MOODS

MINIATURES

AND

MOODS

BY

G. S. STREET

LONDON
Published by DAVID NUTT
in the Strand
1893

NOTE

These are miniatures which are mainly the outcome of a mood and moods which are indicated in miniature. They were published in 'The National Observer,' and are republished by the editor's kind permission, and with a few trifling alterations. The writer hopes they have consistency of criticism and coherence of thought enough to acquit him of impertinence in collecting them.

CONTENTS

Miniatures

Moods

CONTENTS

MINIATURES

A

AN OLD REPROBATE

THE gospel of hard work, the half-crown start, laborious days, comfortable preferment finally or popular acclamation—these things are complacently recorded by elderly mediocrities in many a hulking tome. There are other things in life, and it may be you sometimes pause in your painful striving after perfection to think of them. Then are your thanks due to the wicked and garrulous Chevalier Grammont, who observed the ways of your fathers when a merry monarch was scandalous and poor; to the accomplished Anthony Hamilton, who recorded his observations; to Sir Walter (needing no epithet), who edited a translation of them; and to the serviceable Bohn, by whom or in whose spirit a revised edition has been issued.

The revision need not trouble you. Very like you do not care though 'the prettiest and worst actress in the kingdom,' Rochester's protégée, is found to have been Sarah Cooke and not Mrs. Barry. Your limitations shall be cared for ; we will keep—more or less—to the theme. And, indeed, if we were to follow our Chevalier very closely, reasons other than the quality of your complaisance would bar the way. Alas, and alack-a-day ! It is well known the book is not *virginibus puerisque*. A persecuted poet complained twenty-five years ago of the casting from the library of ' all that cannot be ' lisped in the nursery or fingered in the school- ' room ' : let his arguments absolve the service- able Bohn ; as for you and me, excursions and alarums give us headaches. Yet is it permitted to observe that—apart from details—the com- plete lack of morals in the tone of Grammont has a refreshing quality such as Lamb found in Wycherley and Congreve. Thus, when the jealous Lord Chesterfield, who had been edu- cated in the South, carried off his wife from a dangerous Court, ' This,' says Grammont, ' made all the mothers vow to God that none ' of their sons should ever set a foot in Italy.' And when the lady summoned her lover Hamilton (not Anthony, you are pleased to remark) to her country house, only to laugh at him for his pains, the Chevalier is indig- nant. It is merely a harmless affectation ; to talk of the hypocrisy of cynicism is an unsea- sonable heaviness. And it is good to remem- ber that the end of all the Chevalier's errors was that he won to honourable marriage the beautiful Mistress Hamilton (this edition commits the detestable anachronism of 'Miss'), and lived to a good old unrepentant age.

There are points in this book for patriotic pride. To begin with, it was written by a Briton (he was Scots by his father's, Irish by his mother's, side) in a style of French that won Voltaire's praise. Next, Grammont, versed in the ways of the Court of Louis xiv., and long restored to it, speaks still in his old age with enthusiasm of the Court of Charles ii. We are over ready to think of that time as one of disgrace merely in our annals; we can spare a word, now and then, for its wit and its art. Of the politeness of the Court, the fineness of the town, and above all the charms of the women, Grammont, even if you allow for Anthony's patriotism, is an honest eulogist. Mrs. Hyde—she was sister-in-law to the Duchess of York, and 'little Jermyn' made her famous—had 'a foot surprisingly beautiful ' even in England.' And Frances Stewart ' possédoit cet air de parure . . . qu'on n'attrape ' guère à moins que de l'avoir pris en France dès ' sa jeunesse'; still Frances Stewart was not a Frenchwoman. Her story, by the way, is a puzzle to the sagacious (our dear Chevalier sets an example of discursiveness). She was for long a pre-eminent, but—say the historians— an innocent beauty of the Court, and then she

married the Duke of Richmond, whose scene
with Charles is famous. The erudite Edmund
Lodge is enthusiastic about her virtues; and
yet she seems to have taken advantage of an
amorous but not tyrannical master, to have
calculated on the death of a kind mistress
(whereby she might have been—who knows?
—Queen in her stead), and more than another
to have broken that Queen's heart. Very
likely she was virtuous; but may one not
prefer poor Nelly? Many a curious picture is
given here. My Lord of Rochester, banished
from court, sets up in Tower Street as a famous
'German doctor,' and establishes a thriving
practice. How two maids-of-honour, disguised
as orange wenches, went in search of this
famous doctor, and what befell them by the
way, let our author tell. He is immoral,
trivial, and—as himself said of Buckingham—
the father and mother of scandal. Yet he is
worth reading. His intellect is various. For
a while he trifles; then he gives you an
example of his insight, saying of Arlington
that 'his great earnestness passed for business, his impenetrable stupidity for secrecy';
anon he assures you easily, like Tacitus, that
'the public grows familiar with everything by
'habit.' Assuredly it had need in those days.
You read here with interest the gay stories of
Charles and his friends; you frown, but the

taste is not altogether bad. Granted the tone of these men and women was vicious, and the lives of them useless. Yet they had wit among them, and a more general love of art than has been known often at Court, and a love of sport. Beneath some complexity of manner there was great simplicity of essence. You loved, and were accepted altogether or rejected. You married, and your wife was faithful—or not. A time of decisive blows, to die of or recover from. You have an idea that such things as the Chevalier relates 'hurt not the heart nor the brain.' They did not then analyse and curse their birth in corners. Complexity is development, some tell us; but there is happiness of a kind in this simplicity which you find, at the bottom, in Grammont, with much wit and food for more reflection.

ZIMRI THE WRITER

WE have it from one who had scant reason to love him that George Villiers was 'all mankind's epitome.' But with Buckingham, the builder, chemist, art-patron, epicure, man-killer, woman-killer, musician, politician, we are not here concerned. Our theme is Buckingham the writer.

You think, or ought to think, at once of *The Rehearsal.* Reading it to-day, one feels of course a slowness and slightness of appreciation; for who has read *The Lost Lady, Pandora, The Slighted Maid,* and the rest of the plays it caricatures, even though some six of them (as *Granada, Marriage-à-la-Mode,* and *Love in a Nunnery*) were Dryden's own? The key may help you to understand the parody of the letter; but it was the spirit of the heroic drama that Buckingham set out to laugh away, and that is evaporated. He was writing for a small audience, mostly of inveterate playgoers;

8

an audience saturated with this spirit and quick to take his points. But the early demand for a key shows that the allusions easily became obscure. One's enjoyment of *The Critic* is far more facile, though Sheridan's play has less body and wit than this one, and Puff is a more shadowy creation than Mr. Bayes. And yet Bayes is made up of two originals; a fact explained by a somewhat curious circumstance. It is said that *The Rehearsal* took ten years to write (and, by the way, that the Duke's was not the only hand in it); and in the beginning d'Avenant, Poet Laureate, and chief of the Duke of York's Company, was to hand for ridicule; and the incident of the patched nose is clearly a relic of the first conception: you remember d'Avenant's nose in *Woodstock*? But Dryden, whose light was shining high before the ten years were out, was a worthier object, and so the part was altered to fit him, and Buckingham was careful to instruct Lacy the player in personal imitation. The effect of fretful vanity and fatuous complacency is admirable. And though Buckingham was attacking a man whose poetic little finger was thicker than his own loins, his particular intent was sane. Those luckless Puritans may have been responsible (as Dryden affirms) for the inception of the heroic plays, but the fustian and bad art of these are at least as remarkable as their poetry. One can understand that their iteration was a nuisance. Unfortunately, satire is rarely discriminating, and some of the passages parodied were a credit to their authors. Such incidents, on the other hand, as the caricature of the two letters in *The Virgin Widow* by the two boots are in the true vein. For the rest, *The Rehearsal* is curiously minute, robust, and pleasant, a remorseless study of cheap effects. And one only remembers, as a rule, the 'two Kings of Brentford,' who are a slight and unessential part of its mechanism.

The Rehearsal, then, is a thing apart, appealing to an accidental but a special experience, and hard to be otherwise appraised, as is all caricature, from Aristophanes his *Frogs* to the fun they made t'other day of Mr. Oscar Wilde, between which two one may place it for obscurity and wit. The other plays have one general characteristic : they bear the marks of work done by a man of great ability who was unpractised in his medium. They are somewhat crude, that is, and somewhat fine ; there is much of the amateur in them and nothing of the fool. The sum of indecency in them, as in the few poems we have, is small ; they are rather frank than gross. Surely (this by the way) only a race essentially indelicate

could have invented a delicacy that consists
merely in ignoring the common facts of physical existence—a delicacy to be acquired with
ease by the coarsest and most vulgar mind
in the world, and one that is in itself a mode
of coarseness. Buckingham was of a society
indubitably refined in some directions, and as
indubitably free-spoken; and as, when he
wrote, he kept what we call indecency in
natural perspective and due proportion, he is,
therefore, blameless in that respect. There
is some brightness in *The Chances.* 'To the
' King's house to see *The Chances.* A good
' play I find it, and the actors most good in it.
' And pretty to hear Knipp sing in the play
' very properly "All night I weepe"; and sung
' it admirably. The whole play pleases me
' well: and most of all, the sight of many fine
' ladies: among others . . .' Mr. Pepys was
an impressionist critic. The blank verse of
The Restauration: or Right will take place; A
Tragi-Comedy, is for the most part indefensible.
Now and again the sentiment impresses:
' (death) is but the giving up a Game which
' must be lost' is one of those commonplaces
that wisdom feels and cleverness contemns;
and in another place the old idea of Canute
and the waves is admirably expressed. The
view of tragi-comedy is indeed more primitive than Mr. Meredith's, the comedians and

tragedians being distinct; yet nor tragedy nor
comedy is below a fair level. *Sedgmoor* and
The Militant Couple need not detain you; the
one is a slight personal squib, the other a
study of unhappy tempers in action before
analysis was familiar. The poems are more
interesting. There is no poetry in them,
none; but there is a pertinent, a full-blooded
kind of wit that a man should relish. *The
Instalment*—trivial in subject—is spirited from
beginning to end, and so are most of the
others. The *Consolatory Epistle to Captain
Julian the Muses' Newsmonger* is a faint fore-
shadow of *The Dunciad*, though a world less
malignant.

> 'Thus while our Bards are famished by their
>   Wit,
> Thou, who hast none at all, yet thriv'st by it,'

was worth the quoting, for the story is as new
as it was old. A line in another set of verses—
'All True Love is grounded on Esteem'—
comes passing queerly (to let Buckingham the
man intrude) from him whose mistress held
his horse while he killed her husband; but
that emotion plays ancient tricks yet with our
intellects.

The fantastic imagination that spoiled in a
worldly sense George Villiers' active life and
excited the groundlings' widest gape plays,

you see, an insignificant part in his literary remains. And when you come to read his speeches in Parliament and a few of his letters you are struck with their clear reasoning and business-like plainness. They are put forcibly, of course; but there are no inapposite flights of fancy. In matters of policy he was all for logic, and his failure as an artist therein is merely that logic is of all things detested by the average politician: his assumption of untrue premises was only a part of the game. And in matters of faith he was all for reason: '. . . when the first heat (of the Reformation) ' was over, and considering Men began to ' reflect, that the Reformation offered nothing ' but words . . . they saw no satisfactory ' motive for quitting their old *Mumsimus* for a ' new *Sumsimus*, and could find no real advan- 'tage in withdrawing from Father Peter to ' Father Martin, and Father John, since tho' ' these disclaimed the Infallibility the others ' usurpt, yet they still, without that Guard, ' demanded our Belief of their Doctrines, tho' ' not less absurd and ridiculous.' It sounds trite nowadays, but serves to show his range as a writer, various in that as in all things. In fine, one cannot reckon his merits as writer without a glance at the rest of him. It is poor philosophy, for many an author known for his authorship alone has dissipated his energies in a hundred other directions. But you cannot choose but say that Buckingham, as a writer virile, witty, immature, is great among statesmen and wastrels who have written.

'THAT DEIL O' DUNDEE'

THERE are few more pleasant or more bracing emotions than honest indignation, and it can be enjoyed in double measure by whoso will carefully study the fate of John Graham of Claverhouse. Not his fate in the flesh, for that was glorious: if his service was toilsome, it was rewarded as he wished; he played the game, and knew not the bitterness of losing it. But his fate, as he has fared at the hands of historians, is otherwise and very curious to follow. You may first read Macaulay with his extracts from his Covenanting authorities (Walker and Wodrow and the rest), and enjoy your first possession of wrath; you pity the poor Covenanters and rail at the cruelties of their wicked oppressor, who 'shed the blood of the saints like water.' And then you may read Napier's Memorials and Letters, and rejoice worthily at the exposure of the fanatics who calumniated a hero, and of the illustrious and popular historian who copied with gleeful facility those lies about a man, his equal (very probably) in intellect, and vastly his superior in most other things.

It is all old history now. Truth is great and has prevailed over Lord Macaulay, whose word nobody would now take by itself. But the matter is still worth a few sentences. In the first place, Napier's book is excellent good reading. He writes frankly as a hater of the side he is attacking, as an amateur, and, one may say, as a sportsman. He does not affect to be cool ; his indignation is roused, and he rouses yours inevitably in stating a case whose strength is not in the remarks of a hot partisan (as we may fairly call him) but in the nature of things and in authentic documents. It is very pleasant to follow him as he exposes, indignantly but humorously, the deliberate ignorance of Macaulay, and makes sport of the crazy reveries of Wodrow and Patrick the Pedlar and the rest of the saintly historians, and proves to you the cowardly maliciousness of Bishop Burnet. And he is ever careful and ready with his evidence ; in fact, he is a wholesome corrector of 'that rapid, dazzling, and 'dramatic history, which so often delights us 'in Lord Macaulay and the Christmas panto-'mimes.' In the second place, truth has had in this instance a weightier adversary than the Whig champion. For tens that have read Napier, hundreds have read Macaulay, but

thousands *Old Mortality*.   That Sir Walter
with his Tory principles and his Cavalier sympathies should have painted Claverhouse, the
hero of Killiecrankie, blacker than he was, is
strange indeed.   But we must remember that
the Covenanters, their piety and pathos and
saintliness and sufferings, were become a sort
of national myth, whose influence was hard
to withstand.   The result is one of his few
failures, a character that merely as a creation
of fiction is impossible.   None of us is wholly
black or white ; all are grey, as we know.   But
this Claverhouse in *Old Mortality* combines
qualities that may hardly co-exist : a gentleman cannot be deliberately cruel towards
inoffensive people.   Either the character is
impossible, or one must say that, as Sir Walter
draws it, his eulogistic remarks are, on
analysis, valueless.   But in truth he was thinking of the ' Christian Carrier.'   The story of
this worthy, how he was peaceably gardening,
when ' bloody Clavers ' came upon him, and
for no particular reason, except that he (Brown
was his name) was virtuous, shot him with his
own hand, and went on to gibe at his widow,
who had seen the ghastly outrage—this, all
this is told with the greatest unction by Peter
the Pedlar.   Sir Walter had seen the account,
and had not seen a then unpublished letter,
which shows that Brown was a rebel, in hiding

since Bothwell Bridge and engaged in foment-
ing sedition ; that he was found in possession
of arms, and executed by the ordinary law of
the time. One feels sure there was something
shady about a person called 'the Christian
Carrier.' Pity Sir Walter accepted the story.
He wrote afterwards : '. . . the beastly
'Covenanters, against whom he (Dundee) acted,
'hardly had any claim to be called men unless
'what was founded on their walking upon
'their hind feet. You can hardly conceive
'the perfidy, cruelty, and stupidity of these
'people, according to the accounts they have
'themselves preserved.' Still, he leaves his
Claverhouse a cross between the 'bloody
Clavers' of the Covenanters and the 'Bonnie
Dundee' of his own immortal song ; and he
can scarce have seen those letters which the
Duke of Buccleuch allowed Napier to publish.

The fact, of course, is that the Covenanters
were impossible citizens, whom the Government of Charles II. (it may be at least argued)
was justified in suppressing. It was all very well
to call it tyranny to prevent their 'worshipping
God in their own way,' but that way included,
among other things, the murder of an old
archbishop in the arms of his daughter—a more
authentic person than the Christian Carrier's
widow. The Government and their worthiest
instrument determined to crush them once

and for all.   Claverhouse could not have liked
the work; but, as he writes, 'I am as sorry to
'see a man die, even a Whig, as any of them-
'selves; but when one dies justly for his own
'faults, and may save a hundred to fall in
'the like, I have no scruple.'   He was severe,
then, terribly severe by our idea, and was
perhaps the executant of a bad policy; but
severity is not cruelty.   His stirring life was
of the kind to call out a man's working
virtues.   In his prosecution of the Covenanters
he showed unequalled energy and vigilance;
at Court tact and fascination; at the fall of
James statesmanship and genius in war; and
throughout his life, in his early service with
the Prince of Orange in his youth as at Killiecrankie, unqualified personal courage.   These
qualities one may predicate of him for certain.
They raise some questions: he was almost the
only bold and loyal adviser near James's person when William landed, and one wonders
if, had James listened, he would then, or
later in Scotland, have driven the Dutchmen
into the sea.   It was quite possible.   But still
better for his fame and for posthumous sympathy to die as he died.   'One named John-
'ston told the deponent that he had catched
'the Viscount as he fell from his horse, after
'his being shot, at the said fight; the Viscount
'then asking the said Johnston how the day

'went, and that he answered—the day went
'well for the King—meaning King James,
'but that he was sorry for his lordship; and
'that the Viscount replied—it was the less
'matter for him, seeing the day went well for
'his Master.' *Dulce et decorum est.* But these
qualities do not exhaust his character. He
was polished, of course, and that rapid success
at Court of a country gentleman who had passed
his life in the field is sufficiently impressive;
but he had learning as well. His spelling is
that of his time, but his expression is ready,
and shows at least a clear head and a capable
intellect. With every beauty, he was not
amatory. In spite of his writing once that he
would take a certain lady 'in her Smoak'—
she was not to be taken—one may say he was
somewhat cold in this relation, and, if even his
Covenanting critics had not borne witness to
his morals, that he had gone fast and was
tired. Being in treaty for the daughter of a
Presbyterian house, he writes to one who
feared bad influences for him : 'It is not in the
'power of love, nor any other folly, to alter
'my loyalty.' Poor man, he was sorely tried :
having to leave his wife on his wedding-day to
go and suppress a conventicle or some such
meeting; and he allowed himself a rare expression of irritation : 'I shall be revenged some
'time or other of this unseasonable trouble

' those dogs give me. They might have let ' Tuesday pass.' Loyalty was his passion, and his passion, as that of others like him, has often been written of as though there were something stupid and wrong-headed about its persistence. But it may be that in his day loyalty to King James was the creed of an enlightened statesman ; that the stupidity was, if anywhere, with those who would call in a foreigner to prevent an universal toleration.

One takes his leave of Dundee with admiration : a strong, capable, masculine man, severe even to extremity in the interests of what he thought just and conducive to the nation's happiness ; planning his own advantage as an honest man may ; clear-headed at the supreme crisis, daring and loyal to death. It is worth noting that, a few fanatics apart, the counsel for the other side is only Bishop Burnet, who cringed to the powers that were and told lies about them when they were not —him and none other. For Macaulay took his lies ready-made.

ROCHESTER

O a certain order of mind the contemplation of a laborious and useful life, ending full of years and deserved honours, though that life be coloured by commanding abilities, has less of attraction in it than the memory of a genius on whom, after a brief period of fitful dazzling, the gods have put the seal of their love. It is odd, then, that Rochester, who died in his thirty-fourth year, confessed pre-eminent in wit by the universal judgment of his time, and eulogised for it by a critic so antipathetic to his failings as Dr. Johnson—Rochester, the hero of so many adventures desperately wicked—should be known to most readers to-day only for a couple of moderate epigrams on Charles the Second. His coarseness occurs at once to your mind; but that can be matched in many a well-known author—in Catullus, for example, read in schools and furnished with one of the most elaborate and learned commentaries in the record of English scholarship. In the

matter of circumstantial excursions on for
bidden ground Rabelais beats him to nothing-
ness. Not mere coarseness is the reason, but
the fact that Rochester chooses almost invari-
ably as his material subjects whose mention is
offensive to our manners. Had he but smeared
a page with ribaldry here and there, a common
pair of scissors had secured him permanence.
But in truth—be it that an obsession of such
things was the cause, or an enjoyment of
amused deprecation, or (but this is not likely)
a lower pride in his daring—effects and motives
on which we have agreed to silence are his
usual themes; so that if you remove the
coarseness you leave nothing behind—or rather
his poem upon Nothing (and one or two more),
which Johnson calls his strongest effort.
There one may suppose with deference that
the Doctor was misled by his chaste mind;
for, in spite of some well-sounding lines, the
thing is but a frigid result of easy ingenuity.
It is rather in some of his least fastidious
attempts that you find exceeding good wit,
sense, and pungency; and should there come
a time when all natural things shall be free of
mysterious evil and reproach, so that pruriency
shall be impossible and coarseness motiveless,
a time when—most like it will never be—all
fields shall be playgrounds for art without
exception, then the dog will have his day.

For 'in all his works,' says Johnson, 'there is 'spriteliness and vigour, and everywhere may 'be found tokens of a mind which study might 'have carried to excellence.' It is not, of course, merely a tolerance which will allow any subject to be mentioned that is required of him who would read this author, but one which will grant any subject to laughter and gibes; an absolute equality of subjects must be premised. Now and again there is a note of self-mocking pathos, and sometimes of a *sæva indignatio* that reads curiously real, as in the Satire on Charles, 'for which he was banished the Court.' And in some of his attacks on his enemies there is a quite refreshing power of abuse. But do not run to read Rochester, for he is beyond all conception ribald. By the way, he is hard to get at, and the authenticity of some of the poems even in the early editions is doubtful. Even in his own day, says Bishop Burnet, anything extraordinary in the way of satire was laid at his door.

The man's life is of more interest than his writings. Even his friends in those merry times deplored his excesses. In preaching his funeral sermon, a sort of composition not over exact as a rule, the worthy clergyman remarks: 'From the breasts of his Mother, 'the University, he first sucked those Perfec-

'tions of Wit, Eloquence, and Poetry, which
'afterwards by his own corrupt Stomach or
'some ill Juices after, were turned into Poison,
'to himself and others.'   St.-Evremond in that
letter to the Duchess of Mazarine in which he
places Rochester above Boileau as 'nearest the
ancients in Satire,' yet, remarking that he
was born in the year of Charles the First's
martyrdom, adds the unkind reflection : 'The
'King was fitter for the world to which he
'went from the Scaffold than his Lordship for
'that he entered into from his Mother's
'Womb.'   As for our friends Evelyn and
Pepys, the one calls him 'a very prophane
wit,' the other 'an idle rogue.'   (You may
dig out of the last-named gossip a story of
how my lord ran away with and married Mistress Mallet, 'the great beauty and fortune of
the North.'   'A melancholy heiress,' Grammont calls her, but says nothing of the elope-
ment.)   And Johnson finishes him with
customary thunder : 'Thus in a course of
'drunken gaiety and gross sensuality, with
'intervals of study perhaps yet more criminal'
—surely that is passing hard—'with an avowed
'contempt of all decency and order, a total
'disregard to every moral and a resolute
'denial of every religious obligation, he lived
'worthless and useless, and blazed out his
'youth and his health in lavish voluptuousness.'

In truth he was a mass of contradictories. Distinguished for personal bravery in the Dutch war—at Bergen he took a message from one ship to another in an open boat, hotly fired on the while—he lived to gain a reputation for cowardice in private quarrels. It is just possible that a life to undermine the nerves may not have been the reason for this so much as a contempt for public opinion pushed to an extreme ; in the spirit of his own saying that 'every man would be a coward if he durst.' Again, he was often indifferent to the advances of Court beauties, but he would go to an infinity of trouble (as in the famous Newmarket story) for a low amourette. And—one is almost sorry for it—he affords the common spectacle of the rake repentant on his death-bed, if one may trust Dr. Burnet, who to be sure had something to gain by the conversion of so notorious a sinner. He showed then that moral weakness which attributes vices to unhappy opinions : declaring, according to Parsons, that he owed his undoing to Hobbes' philosophy !

But neither these deploring clergymen nor his eulogistic friends appear to have found the secret of his life. It was the passion for acting. The stories of his strange disguises, his habit of going among all classes, speaking their language and adopting their manners, and above all his grand *coup* of setting up as a quack-doctor—('Alexander Bendo's speech' is excellent reading)—show the histrionic instinct. Now he would be a brave soldier, and now the sturdy patriot, lashing the vices of the Court and hurling his satires and epigrams at the King's mistresses—at Portsmouth and Cleveland who deserved them, at Mrs. Gwynn who did not. And, by the way, he was generally, says St.-Evremond, 'in contradiction to the Town' in his dramatic judgment; 'and ' in that, perhaps, he was generally in the ' right, for of all audiences in polite nations ' perhaps there is not one that judges so very ' falsely of the Drama as the English.' Good St.-Evremond, had you but lived to-day!

No, you can hardly tell the secret of this complex life. Perhaps it was an insatiable curiosity: the man, for no earthly reason you can think of, set detectives to note him the indiscretions of the Court. Perhaps—perhaps the artificial elegy on him of Mistress Behn was all he deserved :

'Mourn, mourn ye Muses all ; your loss deplore :
The young, the noble Strephon is no more';

and so forth. But Rochester was a man of genius, was (he said) drunk for years together, and died of old age at thirty-three. And yet there is no cult of his memory.

MY LORD JUDAS

OOM for a rogue ! It should be accorded readily, for rogues are mostly an interesting folk, and this one's roguery was naturally daring and persistent, and perfected by art withal. And yet, to be frank, there is that in the story of the second Lord Sunderland from which one turns repelled and sickened. For, making a conventional distinction between common honesty and traditional honour, one may affirm of the amiably disposed that, while offences against the former may amuse them, they cannot away with a violation of the latter code. You would, for example, consent to listen to the experiences of a capable rascal sentenced for forgery, or at least to read them; but would not your interest in human nature need great strength to repress the protest of your instinct, were you required to study—say a Denzil Somers who took a pension of Sir Austin and bullied Lady Feverel? The natural history of such an one is unpleasant, but sometimes wholesome to set forth.

As thus: if we believe certain evidence against him, my Lord Sunderland's failings were lying, ingratitude, and treachery. But this evidence has been treated very discreetly, lest it cast a shadow on the glories of the Revolution; for without a treacherous Minister (our subject) at Whitehall and a treacherous Minister (his uncle, Henry Sidney) at the Hague, the path of the knot of intriguers who upset the second James had been thorny, possibly even to despair. And so it is related by Lodge that when Addison suggested to Edmund Smith a history of the Revolution, the complacent essayist and Whig secretary was vastly disturbed by the question: 'What shall I do with the character of Lord Sunderland?' It disposed of the scheme, for only one answer was given by facts known to all the world. Nobody could deny that Sunderland, then professing Roman Catholicism, had been the chief abettor, and probably instigator, of James in that treatment of the Church of England which was the lever used for his expulsion; that he was not dismissed from office until William had set sail; that he had taken refuge in Holland, of all places, from asserted fear of the new king; and that, returning presently to England, he was only kept out of office by the disgust of popular opinion and jealousy of rivals. It seems likely enough that while

James's Minister, being in correspondence, through his uncle, with William, he had deliberately encouraged his master in a course that he knew would end in his ruin. James was, as has been shown, since Macaulay's day, an enlightened and intelligent man; but he was altogether unappreciative of the native Conservatism of his subjects, and one sees how his intellect and temperament were an easy prey to a subtle and experienced counsellor, who could read the signs of the times. But one only appreciates the full magnificence of Sunderland's treachery when one remembers that he had voted for James's exclusion in 1680, had turned about and fawned, and been taken into favour—with the Stuart incapacity for long resentment—honoured and caressed. Add then the fact that he had been throughout accepting a pension from Louis, and your completed picture of complex rascality will surely try your power of disgusted admiration.

These are the excuses for relating facts by no means obscure or in need of great research. The stating of them, even though it be *crambe repetita* to you, is in sort a homage to truth, which has been little courted in this particular, and the junction of attraction by what is intellectual with repulsion by what is moral in the same acts may be possibly a curious sensation. As a rule, what repels is irrelevant to what attracts—the case of a wife-deserting poet, for instance—or else is merely an offence against honesty; here the two are apprehended together. And though one would not call Sunderland a genius, yet he was so eminent an artist in rascality, his ingenuity was so brilliant and ready, that you cannot choose but admire, and wish there had been in his case some element—some passion of desire or revenge— to make him less contemptible a man. If you accept the hostile version of Sunderland's conduct in the Monmouth rebellion, it is hard to enjoy the grand simplicity of his plan and the coolness of its execution without the intruding contempt for his vile treachery. Our morality will impertinently obscure artistic appreciation! It was so admirable, when Monmouth had implicated him, to assure him of pardon if he should not confess, and then, having destroyed his credit by making him contradict himself, to intercept his letter to the king, and so get him despatched with all speed. But is it, or is it not, an affectation to maintain that its vileness does not destroy your pleasure?

A remark or two may be added to this miniature in words. That he is said by Evelyn to have impoverished himself by play is by comparison to his credit. He married a daughter of Digby, Earl of Bristol; but Mr. Pepys heard of an odd incident of the court-

ship. 'The wedding clothes were made, and
' portion and everything agreed on and ready;
' and the other day he goes away nobody yet
' knows whither, sending her the next morning
' a release of his right or claim to her, and
' advice to his friends not to inquire into the
' reason of this doing, for he hath enough of
' it; and that he gives them liberty to say and
' think what they will of him, so they do not
' demand the reason of his leaving her, being
' resolved never to have her.' But they were
well matched, she being an ambitious woman
and disliked of her husband's mother, the
gentle Sacharissa. Even so; this was the son
of none other than Dorothy Sidney, the model
of wifely constancy and the best inspiration of
Waller, whose prophecies for her happiness
were so cruelly falsified—all of them save that
she would live long, which, poor woman, she
might well have wished had not come true. It
was ill for Sunderland that his simple-hearted
and loyal father died at Newbury for his king
so young; one can fancy Sacharissa was not
the best regent for his disposition, that she
made him too absolute a prince. He is said
to have been quick at his books as a boy, and
to have matured his talents and accomplish-
ments by a lengthened stay abroad. We know
how he used them: to advance himself to
highest place, and to support him in an ex-

tremity of unscrupulous daring, and to leave
his memory so patently vile that the bare
mention of his name shocked Mr. Addison.
It is a comfort to reflect that he overreached
himself, and that William could not altogether
defy the opposition to his reinstatement.
' April 24 (1691).   I visited the Earl and
' Countess of Sunderland, now come to kiss
' the king's hand, after his return from Hol-
' land. This is a mystery. . . . 1 Dec. (1695).
' I dined at Lord Sunderland's, now the
' great favourite and underhand politician,
' but not adventuring on any character, being
' obnoxious to the people for having twice
' changed his religion.'   So he was left to add
to the Althorp Library, already famous, and
be employed worthily in his last days.   To
blame is unphilosophical and to be catholic
the necessary quality; but here is one whose
villainy somewhat jars on your sympathies,
and for once you will not grudge a common
moralist his edification.

c

ETHEREGE

WHEN you read Wycherley, you recognise a master of theatrical effects, the able exponent of a robustly vile humanity; then you feel a trifle sickened, and anon are downright bored. He is no cynic, not held by any ethical convention; if in his pages the world be a thing grotesque, obscene, it is because to a modern apprehension the man was even so: honest he was, as well, and, therefore, with little satisfaction for a splenetic mood. Congreve, of course, is pre-eminent in wit and diction; and because there is a malicious subtlety in the wickedness of his world, and his way is to see evil in everything, while you are aware, all the time, that your author has in reality as clear a perception of what is otherwise as your own, he suits your occasional spite against dull circumstance. But this convention—that there is nothing good under the sun, that desire is the whole of life—grows,

in spite of Elia, tedious to minds that have
outgrown the counter convention of Puritan
propriety too long for constant militancy
against it.

If this be so with you, Etherege should find
place in your appreciations. If he lack the
scenic sense of Wycherley, he lacks also his
brutality; if the wit of Congreve, Congreve's
conscious narrowness. He is more apt to distinguish than either; the passions of his men
take an individual air; his women, honest or
not, show degrees and differences. A most
readable play is his last, *The Man of Mode, or
Sir Fopling Flutter.* It seems to show you
'Gentle George's' world, as he saw it. A
world gayer and more wanton than our own,
but not immersed in (what you would call)
immoral pursuits, not unknowing of the charm
of frank innocence and virile friendship. It
is an obvious criticism to say, with Lamb, that
the whole business of this world is intrigue.
But these plays are frankly of intrigue, and in
what age have idle young men of the town
not given the most of their attention to one
or other sort of the world of women? The
Dorimant is said to be sketched from Rochester, and it may well be the case, though it is
curious that a song in the play, said to be by
Dorimant, is by Sir Charles Sedley. Dorimant
is of profligate habit and ironical temper, a

'fine gentleman,' a man of parts withal, and
fascinating at will. 'I know he is a devil,' says
poor Mrs. Loveit; 'but he has something of the
angel yet undefac'd in him.' Now when he
would cast off this Mrs. Loveit—a woman 'in
society'—it is to be noted that, vain and
unfeeling though he be, he yet sets about it
with a regard for outward decency, bears him
in fact more as a gentleman than in a like
case the hero of *The Story of the Gadsbys*. And
his friend Medley, 'the spirit of scandal'—
said to be Sedley or Etherege himself—and
young Bellair are possible. Old Bellair would
be no doubt accounted coarse in his speech
to-day, but he is neither a brute nor a bully,
and his heartiness (that most difficult quality
to portray) has a certain engaging sincerity.
Sir Fopling Flutter was said by Dean Lockitt
to be Etherege, which can hardly be the case;
the foundation for the idea is that in him
French modes and predilections are ridiculed,
and Etherege had lived in Paris. He may or
may not be drawn from one Beau Hewit, but
in any case he is drawn with art, effectively.
Dryden can say with truth in his epilogue that
'Sir Fopling is a fool so nicely writ, the ladies
' would mistake him for a wit.' His folly is
absurd but not extravagant; his conceit immense but not abnormal. Supposed to have
birth and breeding, he is no clown : and be-

cause it is comedy, the satire is not a whit less mordant. The women are, one passionate and reckless, one amorous and discreet, besides two lightly sketched match-makers. Their superficial coarseness is of the time, hardly more pronounced than you find it a hundred years later.

Of the other two plays, *She Would if She Could* is merely farcical on broad lines, diverting sometimes, sometimes wooden; and *Love in a Tub* is a compound of serious scenes in verse, and of buffoonery dragged in by the heels. They deserve a word: the 'Poems' do not, and one may pass to a general and somewhat noticeable consideration. The girls in Etherege are commonly charming. In the first play, *Love in a Tub*, they are on a poetical plane, and, it may be, dull; but at least you must credit their author with a not ignoble conception. Aurelia, who pleads with her sister to accept the love of a man herself loves secretly, may be unconvincing, but is not, surely, the creation of a narrowly base nature. This play, it is to be observed in the connection, benefited the house by a thousand pounds in a month. In *She Would if She Could* are 'two young ladies' neither prudes nor hussies, neither sticks nor unnaturally witty. Wild by our notions, they are provocative, human, delightful.

'This is sly and pretty,
'And this is wild and witty ;
'If either staid
''Till she dy'd a maid,
'I' faith 'twould be great pity.'

And you feel, as you read, that the catch is in
the right. And Harriet, in the best play, is
likewise natural and frank and charming. All
are unaffectedly aware of the lives of their
suitors, but they are open with their knowledge, and sin not with innuendo or pretence.
And the writers who can show, convincingly,
innocence which is not mere ignorance are
sufficiently uncommon.

Etherege, then, has distinction as a writer.
He is fanciful, life-like, and sometimes even
fine, and is further notable among his contem-
poraries for an effective restraint in satire. A
touch of feeling here and there and a sugges-
tion of romance come pleasantly upon you.
His grossness—ah, there we come on an old
friend in this connection. 'Chastity,' says
Sterne, ' by nature the gentlest of the affections,
' give it but its head—'tis like a ramping and
' a roaring lion.' But it must really spare this
lamb without the argumentative interference
of a champion. Of Etherege the man our
ramping lion has better right to make a meal.
Horace Walpole tells a tale of a king's mistress
discarded, who was insulted by the rabble.

'*Messieurs,*' she said, '*puis-que vous me connoissez, priez Dieu pour moi.*' Etherege was the friend of Rochester, and had to retire with my lord from the public eye. Sent to the Hague by Charles, and to Ratisbon by James, he was a scandalous ambassador given to gaming and other vice. But he had the grace to be ruined by the Revolutions which ruined his master. *Priez Dieu pour lui*, though he himself would not have thanked you.

A VICE-QUEEN

DREAMS will fashion you a concrete result of your knowledge, plain and inferential, that shall exceed in vividness and in convincing truth the utmost imaginings of your waking hours. Should a fairy take you in sleep to England as it was two hundred and a few more years ago, beg that you may talk with her who was Barbara Villiers, Mrs. Palmer, Countess of Castlemaine, and Duchess of Cleveland; for to value her duly you will have to rid you of many prepossessions and associations, not so much of morality as of the accidents of our refinement. If you hunt her through Grammont and the rest, and allow yourself the while to think of the sort of people you know who lead the life of her and her associates, you will fall short of the truth. Much of a wanton will be your verdict, and something of a shrew—a vulgar verdict, be assured. But remember their life was not a revolt against the spirit of society; it was that spirit itself. It is imbecile to doubt (yet a book has been writ to prove) that necessary virtues of the beaver pattern co-existed with that spirit—with the frank offerings of wit and gaiety to the garden-god. But here was the very essence of the interlude in England, and the fact lends a dignity and a different colour to the Court and its Vice-Queen.

One thinks of her as the presiding goddess of what was essential in that Court and makes it memorable in our history. The spirit then ministered clearly to the flesh, and her beauty was fittingly voluptuous. She had beauty and readiness and a sustained gaiety; she was imperious and fearless in self-pleasing. Every atom of delight that life could give her she would have, and have it there and then. And since woman, as we are told, is 'the practical animal,' [it is notable when she throws aside every consideration of prudence for pleasure, and keeps the rewards of prudence until old age. Whatever attracted her she would have. Beauty attracted her, and she made Marlborough. Wit attracted her, and she was the friend of Wycherley and (they said) of Hart, the player. Oddity and spirit attracted her, and she nearly ruined herself for young Jermin. But through it all, power attracted her, and Charles the Second was her slave. She would have all that attracted her, and would therefore deny herself nothing to please him; but if one reads of quarrels and jealousies, one reads always of reconciliations. In truth her sway over Charles was for long almost illimitable—'she hath nearly hectored him out of his wits,' reports Mr. Pepys. One must argue, therefore, a quality of distinctive personality in her, that would not be gainsaid— that rare quality by reason of which some women if once supreme can never be forgotten —for Charles, creature of habit though no doubt he was, was yet of all men easily content with a present impression on his senses, and she had rivals innumerable in that fleshly heart.

Her later amours afford a sight of middle-aged passion as it worked, and that (by the novelist's leave) is more interesting than most young persons' cooing and fluttering. It is then that passion, known for what it is, and not bedecked with deceits about communion of spirit and the like (natural enough to boys and girls, but not, after youth, to the enlightened, for there is a line between passion and affection, though one may sink or rise into the other), it is then that passion is sincere and worthy. 'I love your body, not your soul,' said a middle-aged poet; if this woman was loved for something beside her body, no lover thought the soul angelic.

You see how, in trying to depict her, the pen runs here and there. A few bald epithets are not enough, and the details in the authorities are not worth repeating. (The respectable Evelyn had strong disapproval for her, and Mr. Pepys uplifted his mildly inflammable and honest little soul, and 'loved her very much.') But you see the thoughts that play round the image one has of her. There remains to be said, as memorable, that of the three dukes, her sons, one was a strong man, a good sailor and commander, courageous and decided, of great personal beauty, which he bequeathed from his mother to his line. She died in esteem a quarter of a century after Charles had made his last apology. She stands for her time; selfish, reckless, and full of the joy of living, she looked life in the face and lived one of its lessons.

THE ATALANTIS

T is to be said of Mary Manley that she was the second English-woman who lived by writing, competing professionally with men. The first was, of course, Aphra Behn, her predecessor by not very many years. The outward difference between them is that Mrs. Behn, though a female politician, was one merely of the ancient order of spies, and is remembered as a writer (in biographies and cyclopædias) for her plays and novels, while Mrs. Manley was essentially a political writer, and her memorable *Atalantis* a collection of the fiercest of partisan attacks and eulogies. This fact does, perhaps, decrease her interest for psychology. A woman's intellect differs from a man's in so far as her emotions are distinctively feminine, and in so far as they colour it; and in political writing of that time the whole-hearted love and hatred (that we are told are characteristic of feminine women) had, if he or she did not possess them, to be simulated by man and woman alike. You cannot, therefore,

44

say that you detect the woman when she hits unscrupulously and unmercifully, and praises with almost ludicrous forgetfulness. Moreover, politics apart, the *Atalantis* is not peculiarly feminine. It is not so much indecent (as you may have read) as sensual, and it appeals to the masculine and feminine sensualist pretty evenly. But if you cannot trace the woman in Mrs. Manley's work as a whole, her life was that of many of Eve's daughters in an imperfect society. She loved, and was abandoned, and then she abandoned herself. Whether in a perfect society the former abandonment will be unheard of, or the latter not an almost necessary consequence, who shall say? Mary Manley was left by her father, Sir Robert, to the protection of her cousin, a very villain of melodrama, who went through a form of marriage with her (his wife being alive) and deserted her, having spent her fortune. This is her own account, and she says: ' I had married ' him, only because I thought he loved me; those ' that knew his person will easily believe that ' I was not in love with him.' You need hardly divest yourself of the moral attitude of your time to forgive this poor lady, if she lived afterwards more for pleasure than for virtue. Indeed, you would have no business with her virtue, were it not that the story may help you to see her as she was.

The 'Secret Memoirs and Manners of 'Several Persons of Quality of both Sexes from 'the New Atalantis, an Island in the *Mediter-* '*ranean*,' consists for the most part of a series of outrages on the Duke of Marlborough and his party, interrupted by an occasional passage in praise of her own party—Harley, for instance, or Mrs. Masham. The machinery of the thing is in the beginning elaborate and somewhat clumsy, and is changed for a clumsier in the third volume; but except the necessary change of names there is no attempt to conceal identities, or rather there is every effort to make them known. It would be too long a task, and one probably ungrateful, to take you through her merely political onslaughts; but one must note that on Marlborough, for you can hardly find a more thorough and pitiless exposure. Every one of the wretched incidents of his rise to fortune is painted with every touch malignity could suggest. She is always careful to make her stories interesting and amusing on their merits as stories, and so in this attack, and in that on the Earl of Portland, there is every picturesque detail to stimulate imagination. It will interest you more to be told that when she speaks of her colleagues in letters, she is able to lay aside her politics to the extent of extolling Addison, with, of course, a lament for his evil ways. But you

wonder to hear her praise is for his verse!
Prior shall 'live for ever in his peculiar strain,
his own immortal numbers.' Of poor Mrs.
Behn : '. . . Sapho'—so she spells it—'the
'Younger . . . tho' when living was owner
'of a soul as amorous as the Elder, yet wanted
'much of that delicacy, and all that nice, yet
'daring spirit (of which hers is but a faint
'imitation), so applauded in Phaon's Mistress.'
There are tributes to Wycherley and Congreve,
and a glowing one to Betterton, the player.
'Roscius, a sincere friend and man of honour;
'not to be corrupted, even by the way of living
'and manners of those whom he hourly con-
'versed with; Roscius, born for everything
'that he thinks fit to undertake, has wit and
'morality, fire and judgment, sound sense and
'good nature.' Only on Dick Steele she
pours untempered vitriol. You know his portrait, as it was drawn by Dennis the critic?
It is honey, compared with Mrs. Manley's. 'O
'let me ease my Spleen!'—one must keep
her capitals in this passage—'I shall burst with
'laughter; these are prosperous Times for
'Vice. D'ye see that black Beau (stuck up
'in a pert Chariot), thick-set, his Eyes lost in
'his Head, hanging Eye-brows, broad Face,
'and tallow Complexion? . . . He's called
'Monsieur *le Ingrat*, he shapes his Manners
'to his Name, and is exquisitely so in all he

' does ; has an inexhaustible fund of dissimula-
' tion, and does not bely the county he was
' born in, which is famed for Falsehood and
' Insincerity.' Follows some appreciation of
the writer, with a touch of right criticism :
' Tho' he 's a most incorrect writer, he
' pleases in spight of the faults we see and own.
' Whether application might not burnish the
' defect, or if those very defects were bright-
' ened, whether the genuine spirit will not fly
' off, are queries not so easily resolv'd.'   ' I
' remember him almost t' other day, but a
' wretched common Trooper. . . . His morals
' were loose, his principles nothing but pre-
' tence, and a firm resolution of making his
' fortune, at what rate soever.' . . . But we
have taken Dick out of the pillory long ago.

Swift writes to Stella (June 30, 1711) how
he met Mrs. Manley at ' my lord Peterborow's,'
from whom she was soliciting a pension ' for
' her service in the cause, by writing of her
' Atalantis, and prosecution upon it,' and Sir
Walter Scott has a note on the passage. It
seems that she came to the rescue of her
printer, appeared before the Court of King's
Bench, and took all the blame upon herself.
The work was all invention. Lord Sunderland,
who examined her, pointed out particulars for
which coincidence could hardly account. It
must have been inspiration, said the lady. One

imagines his lordship smiled as he suggested that inspiration was hardly associated with such scandal. There are evil angels as well as good, said the indomitable Mrs. Manley. She was not imprisoned, and, the Tories coming presently into power, was rewarded. She succeeded the Dean in the conduct of the *Examiner*.

It has been said you cannot trace the woman in her works, as a whole; but in places you can. The portrait of Captain Steele gave rise to a pretty quarrel in the *Tatler*, and she finally took refuge in her womanhood and his want of gallantry. And when she has given, as Delia, her relation of her misfortunes, she makes her plaint in what some would think a modern vein. 'The world, truly inexorable, is never ' reconciled! Unequal distribution! Why are ' your sex so partially distinguished? Why is ' it in your power, after accumulated crimes, to ' regain opinion; when ours, too oftentimes ' guilty but in appearance, are irretrievably ' lost?'

One collects the portrait of a woman, witty, observant; true to party, and relentless to its enemies; frail and indomitable, implacable and warm-hearted. And one wishes she were to know alive; for than a strong intellect in a woman's weak nature there is no more interesting thing under heaven.

D

'LORD FANNY'

T is not half-a-century since the memoirs of John, Lord Hervey, were given to the world ; they have become a recognised authority for the early years of George the Second, but one doubts if they are as well known as they should be to them that read for pleasure. For you have in them as close and clever an exposition of the seamy side of human nature as was ever made ; of human nature as it was observed by a man with perfect opportunities for observation at close quarters in high places, a man whose intellectual powers were great, raising him to a clear eminence above those he criticised and above his active self. He was well aware of the value of his ' dirty little politics,' as Horace Walpole described them, and well aware of the quality of his memoirs. But one must do something, and politics and Court intrigues were vastly entertaining, and some of us must write something, and ' I am very sensible what mere ' trifles several things are in themselves which

' I have related, but as I know that I myself
' have had a pleasure in looking at William
' Rufus's rusty stirrup . . . I content myself
' with only relating facts just as I see them,
' without pretending to impute the effects of
' chance to design, or to account for the great
' actions of great people always by great
' causes. . . . The intrigues of Courts and
' private families are still the same game and
' played with the same cards.' In other words,
it was human nature that took his fancy, and
he deals with it in a pleasant way ; with some
of the superficial philosophy of his century,
but with more of the unmalicious malice of the
man of the world, always pointed and bright
and intellectually delicate. The Herveys were
a notable family, and it is pretty certain we
may count Horace Walpole one of them :
Carr, Lord Hervey, who predeceased John his
brother, was his father. Uncle and nephew
have an immense deal in common, and the
difference is for the most part just that between a valetudinarian and a real sufferer,
who had perforce to paint his ' coffin-face'
that it might not shock his acquaintance—to
the great disgust of Thackeray.

Eloquence apart, one marvels that *The Four
Georges* could have been written by the writer
of *Esmond*; that Thackeray was content in them
to sink, if not the artist, at least the impartial

historian, in the semi-clerical moralist. 'There
' is John Hervey, with his deadly smile and
' ghastly painted face—I hate him.' Why? He
was a good friend and the most patient servant
of his Queen, and is of the choicest company of
book-acquaintances. 'The man who wrote the
' story'—of the Queen's death—'had some-
' thing diabolical about him.'   A mountain of
a molehill : if the King, in the midst of his
grief, showed his persistent weakness, if he
had said, ' J'aurai des maîtresses,' and she had
answered, ' Cela n'empêche pas,' was there
aught diabolical in recording it, and need one
suppose the recorder did not feel?   'The
' terrible verses which Pope wrote respecting
' Hervey, in one of his own moods of almost
' fiendish malignity, I fear are true.'   Never
was fear more misplaced.   The terrible verses
charge Hervey with the common sins of a
courtier, with the diet fear of epilepsy com-
pelled, and with being effeminate—'Sporus,'
in fact, or ' Lord Fanny' ; Hervey who won
the ' beautiful Molly Lepell,' who worsted the
Prince of Wales in a lady's favours, who went
out with Pulteney for 'the silly received laws
of customary honour,' as he thought them,
and was nearly killed for his pains.   ' His wit
all see-saw between that and this' is in the
fact the only true line in the whole : he revels
in antitheses which he probably moulded on

Tacitus, whom he loves to quote. How the quarrel began nobody knows; but Hervey was the intimate friend of Lady Mary Wortley, and Pope had written on her the foulest lines addressed to a woman since Catullus fell out with Clodia. One wishes Hervey had been more his equal in the war of words.

Since mention has been made of a modern critic of the memoirs, one cannot choose but say something of the excellent and right honourable John Wilson Croker, to whose zeal we owe their disinterment from Ickworth. A sagacious and painstaking man; but it is amusing to observe his disqualification, his inveterate application of the standards of his own more highly respectable period to the people of another age. Not having seen the ms., one does not know how much is left out of our text; very like it is grossness merely, which may be spared. Dealing with Pope's accusations, 'That more serious defect,' says he, ' which might have been really charged upon ' him—laxity of moral and religious principle' —of which he, Mr. Croker, was a bulwark, ' has ' here altogether—or nearly so—escaped the ' censure of the satirist.' It is very unfortunate, but Pope knew better. As for morals, Hervey's were those of his friends, but he used his wife well, and remained in the affection of his really pious father. Sir Robert Walpole's call more loudly for comment, and are indeed interesting; he was as indifferent to the follies of his women folk as he was to the notoriety of his own, and you may have read in these memoirs a very curious relation of his attitude towards the probably untrue scandal about Sir George Oxenden, curious in itself and for Hervey's satanic little comment. And as for religion, he held the views of Bolingbroke and Walpole and Queen Caroline. A discussion of them would be truly superfluous to-day, and Hervey's ironical way when he refers to such things is quite inoffensive. He must have enjoyed the scene where 'some wise, some ' pious, and a great many busy, meddling, ' impertinent people about the Court,' when the Queen was dying, 'asked in whispers every- ' body they met whether the Queen had had ' anybody to pray by her,' and Sir Robert broke out, to their dismay, with : ' Let this farce be ' played : the Archbishop will act it very ' well.' 'A parcel of black, canting, hypo- critical rascals,' was his sacred Majesty's *obiter dictum* on bishops.

There are two completed portraits in the memoirs, one of Queen Caroline, the other of Sir Robert Walpole—the hero and heroine, one may say, of the time. Thackeray has made the world familiar with the outline of her story—a prolonged patience, as he tells it, under the vagaries and bullyings of her shrewd and common little lord. He thinks it was all for love of his vulgar little person, and you dissent. The reason is clear; she was consumed with love of power, and power she had, being regarded of all men as the chief fount of favour from her husband's accession to her death. She knew the way to lead an obstinate temper and a lower intellect is by nominal compliance, and that it should become a habit, potent even in her last suffering, was natural. She was, for the rest, a woman who could inspire affection or awe at will, liking her position and aware of its artificial quality. A touch or two shows us that : 'Je pris mon ' grand ton de Reine,' she says of her bearing towards an unruly subject; and of another occasion, 'Giving oneself all this trouble is *une bonne grimace pour le publique.*' Her frank hatred of the Prince of Wales, of whom our author writes with confessed animus, may be horrible, but its expression is curiously refreshing to read. Her chief distinction, however, must be that she was a woman to whom her husband would write long letters about his troubles with Madame Walmoden—even telling her to consult about them 'ce gros ' homme [Sir Robert], qui a plus d'expérience, ' ma chère Caroline, que vous dans ces affaires'— could write thus, and remain essentially under

her dominion.   And ' ce gros homme ' himself
is a portent on whose political sagacity it were
impertinent to remark to you.   But the tre-
mendous difficulties of his position are beyond
exaggeration—his position between a bitter
and powerful opposition and a troublesome and
lukewarm support at Court.   It is wonderful,
that sheer force of intellect that could take a
man of broad country tastes and simple vanity,
' an ill-bred ' man too, by Hervey's standard,
safely and triumphantly for so long through
all the disaffection on one side and finessing
on the other that hemmed him in.   But when
the Queen died, he began to totter.

There are these two portraits and a multitude
of lively sketches—of a despised king and a
people's rude wit on him, of wooden-headed
dukes and gay Court ladies, of pitiful squabbles
and pitiless passions, of human nature with its
polish ever wearing off.   And through them
all moves John, Lord Hervey, beautiful and
sick, but not ' diabolical,' knowing himself and
impassively observant, polite, and hated by the
thick-witted, as such men are, with a bitter
tongue for his enemies and good counsel for
his friends.   He should be more widely read.

'DEAR GEORGE'

SELWYN was 'my dear George' to nearly all his world. The fact may seem trivial, but of such matter it is that one's knowledge of him is compact. This knowledge is only to be gained in an unusual fashion. We have a few stories and jokes of him, a very few letters written by him, and a many addressed to him; and yet from these latter we know him far better than we know the most of them that have written and inspired the writing of tomes and tomes. And the knowledge is exceeding pleasant, for there are points of character that enable us to reconstruct a man.

Many people, perhaps, think of Selwyn as Thackeray thought before them: as some one fond of cakes and ale, indifferent to everything, affable to everybody. The first quality belongs to that crude picture of 'the fine gentleman,' so astonishing in *The Four Georges*. There is no hard line to be drawn between business and pleasure; methods of pursuit and the qualities of the pursuer are the important matters. 'Old Q.' worked at his horse-racing as hard as his jockeys or his trainers; George Selwyn gave as much attention to his friends' perplexities as any lawyer to his briefs. He certainly was not idle; that account of his day in town, which his friend Lord Carlisle wrote (Thackeray quotes it as a genuine description), is the merest banter. His love of cakes and ale was proper and not remarkable; and for his gambling—Heaven help us if we feel a witless superiority about *that*! He was embarrassed by it, as is shown by his friends' amusingly lugubrious appeals for settlement; and finding it consumed 'too much time, money and thought,' he quietly gave it up. . . . Indifference to some things is a condition of deep interest in others. Selwyn's was partly an effect of manner; his waking from apparent sleep to say a good thing was a standing entertainment at White's. But indubitably politics bored him (this word was beginning its vogue in his day), and he snored in the House as loudly as Lord North. Yet he was by no means without patriotism, there are answers from comparative strangers to whom he had written as likely to have knowledge of the war with France and the American Colonies. His sleepiness concealed an acute sensitiveness on some points. At Oxford he ran into debt in the ancient Oxonian way, and his distress at his father's ensuing coldness reads genuine. And when, for a freak of irreverence that sounds trivial to-day, Oxford expelled him, while his friends in town 'damned' the University and welcomed him back to his clubs, Selwyn showed evidently the greatest anxiety for reparation of an injustice. And there are several instances later of chafing under mis-understanding: which is not a sign of phleg-matic indolence. As to general affability, Selwyn understood that the habit of a gentle-man is nowhere to give pain if pain can be avoided, and to give pleasure whenever plea-sure can be reasonably bestowed; but his was by no means that worthless affection which is wasted on all the world alike. Rather the opposite. He could hate heartily, as Sheridan knew; 'and I do not agree with you,' writes Gilly Williams, 'in your constant declarations ' that, except three or four people, the rest ' are indifferent to you. Jew or Gentile, in ' all probability you will live among them, and, ' I hope a great while hence, will die among ' them; therefore, for God's sake, live upon as ' good terms as you can, and since you must ' sail in the ship, do not contrive to make ' ninety-nine out of a hundred of the crew, ' your enemies.' There was a strain of melan-choly in Selwyn that this passage illustrates, perhaps; it came out in a curiously morbid way, which is notorious. That keen interest in criminals, executions, and all the details of crime and justice (an odd feature) may possibly be explained in part by a certain weariness of the common elements of life, its stereotyped proprieties and misdemeanours, of 'low life above stairs,' as he said when he went to see *High Life Below Stairs*. 'There is a noble ' miscreant,' writes our friend Williams again, ' in the Coop at Worcester. He has only ' robbed his uncle, who kept him out of charity; ' then fired his house, when the whole family ' was asleep, and ran away with three damsels ' by the light of it.' Truly it is refreshing. Connected with this trait, perhaps, but not to be confounded with it, was Selwyn's interest in death for death's sake, and in tombs and monuments. Of the many stories on this head, you need not grudge to have one repeated; for it shows not merely George's tastes, but also a man who could die pleasantly. ' The next time Mr. Selwyn calls,' said Lord Holland on his death-bed, 'show him up : if I ' am alive I shall be delighted to see him, and ' if I am dead he will be glad to see me.'

Surely only a superficial observer could find this melancholy, with all its oddity, greatly inconsistent with Selwyn's intense affection for children. It is indeed ever the melancholy,

as distinguished from the merely cross-grained,
nature that is most attracted by unstudied
gaiety and fondness. The children of Maria
Gunning, the beautiful Lady Coventry, were
at one time his favourites; at another the
children of Lord Carlisle; and very pleasant
are the full and careful accounts of them his
correspondents sent him. But who was Mdlle.
Fagniani? Jesse, who had seen all the papers
extant, could not tell: the Duke of Queensberry and Selwyn each, he thought, believed
himself her father. How Selwyn brought
her up at first, how the Marchioness Fagniani
and her husband took her from him, how he
went through infinite trouble and put up with
endless slights and ingratitude on her account, and how she was finally restored to him;
these things are sometimes painful even now,
but deeply interesting to read. It should
be remembered, however, that 'Old Q.' was
thought very like her in face, and was, in fact,
accepted as her father by more than one of
Selwyn's own friends. The Rev. Dr. Warner,
in particular, is disgusted with the Duke's
coldness and want of paternal affection; but
he left her £150,000, and one may put the
coldness down to jealousy of Selwyn. Mie
Mie's is indeed a curious story.

It is only left to say that the delicacy of
Selwyn's friendship must have deserved the

confidences he received.   Lord Carlisle's letters
have been compared, somewhat casually, to
Byron's.   They have not a tithe of his kins-
man's wit and power—are, in fact, merely
bright and affectionate and sincere.   But the
writer was clearly a man of character and self-
control, and we have him confiding to Selwyn
a very intimate emotion.   He had a passion
for a married woman (he always leaves the
name blank, but there is no harm in saying
she was Lady Sarah Bunbury, George the
Third's Lady Sarah), and, being an honourable
man who could accept facts, he went abroad
until he could meet her in simple friendship.
In letter after letter he begs Selwyn for news
of her, and (somewhat shyly) to know if she
ever mentioned himself.   He married not long
afterwards, and, let us hope, preserved the
friendship.   And Selwyn never married.   His
friends deride him very freely indeed on
the subject of his indifference to women;
but that is a mystery a hundred years past
solving.

And so much for his character.   It would
be very superfluous to remark on the grace of
the letters, and on their scope; how they tell
of Charles Fox, and the bigamous Duchess of
Kingston, and the murdered Miss Ray.   They
are chiefly charming, perhaps, for their tone
of courteous intimacy; especially when the

writers are women, who begin 'Dear Sir,' as
the custom was, but are absolutely free from
bourgeois stiffness.   But it may be a good deed
to clear Dr. Warner from the amusing, admirably coloured, and wholly unfounded character
of him drawn by Thackeray: 'He is a boister-
'ous, uproarious parasite, licks his master's
'shoes with explosions of laughter and cunning
'smack and gusto, and likes the taste of that
'blacking as much as the best claret in "Old
'Q.'s" cellar.   He has Rabelais and Horace
'at his greasy fingers' ends,' etc. etc.   The
poor man has been dead a century, and his
reputation signifies little; it matters more that
Thackeray, in carelessness or for effect, perpe-
trated a literary outrage.   His notion of a 'fine
gentleman' as a curious beast apart made
him unable to see that in all essentials Warner
was the equal and familiar friend of Selwyn.
He was Selwyn's junior by fifteen years, and
Selwyn was over fifty when their connection
began; it is, therefore, natural he should be
respectful.   But his tone is frank and manly;
he did Selwyn's errands, as Selwyn did everybody's, but he does not scruple to censure his
conduct at times, or his choice of friends, of
Queensberry himself.   Says a contemporary:
'His attachment to literature was unbounded;
'he was moderate to an extreme at the table,
and equally abstemious at the bottle; a book,

' a pipe, and a cheerful conversation, in which
' he eminently excelled, were his supreme
' delight.'   He *had* Horace, and many another
classic, at his fingers' ends: but his fingers
were not greasy.

MOODS

THE PORTRAIT ON THE STAIRS

THIS was a picture I had to pass when I would go to or from my room. Most of the rooms were approached by another staircase, so that I had in some measure an exclusive pleasure in it. There was many another, but at this one I never failed to glance a moment, and increased gradually the time of my contemplation. Then I would think on the meaning of its look, and the story of its subject, as I lay awake o' nights. There were charming people and things in that house, but the picture and I had a relation apart; and it welcomed me, flickering in the candle-light, to dreams at night-time, and bade me good-bye every morrow in the light of the sun. So I came to an intimate acquaintance with this lady, and now we have made our account with one another, she and I. My knowledge is not obscured by facts. For it happened that although I was told of many other portraits in the house, this one was not mentioned to me, and I had the wisdom not to ask. I might have heard she was a good wife and excellent mother, and no more; and this would not have pained me, for it is with her secret history I hold converse. But I might have heard she was discarded and died unhappy, and this would have been a discord in the harmony of spiritual realities; for a selfish woman, as I am sure she was, should have lived prosperously. Of irrelevant facts, then, I have only to tell you these: that she lived in Stuart times, and was painted by a good hand.

The oval of the frame suits her. Her features have not regularity, which often bespeaks stupidity; and you could not, perhaps, have called her beautiful. Her eyes are big and blue-grey, her cheeks have a healthy colour, her mouth is full and red, light brown hair waves in curls above her clear forehead. I do not regret she is only a head and shoulders, for the hands would probably have been painted to a convention. See how facts of any sort at once lead you astray. She is no bouncing woman; her eyes are wide, but not bold; they do not even smile on you, but contemplate merely; not with obvious indifference, again, but with the untroubled readiness of good breeding. If she be amused at your bearing or despise your words, she does not show it; if she be interested in you—well, she has seen

many things in her life, and cannot be effusive;
if she love you, you may look on her mouth
and wait, but she will not show that either to
the eye of the world. The mouth is sensuous,
but your grand passions are not for this lady of
the picture.

When she lived in our world, she was of it,
wholly. And she was pleased it should be on
her side—not in primness or timidity but—
because it ministered to her pleasure. She
neither despised nor feared it; she took it for
its worth, and enjoyed and used it. Of this
world she was, and had no heed of any other.
Religion was to her simply one of this world's
forces and conveniences; she might have persecuted an unbeliever, but always in conscious
consideration of her private aims. And as for
all manner of yearning, it was far from her. It
were pleasant to have seen her reception of
some soul-searcher, born before his day, who
thought to cozen from her sympathy for his
mewlings. Her friends were men; and though
her intelligence excused them from being
prime figures in the puppet show, she demanded
manhood of them. For intelligence she had,
and humour too, and they, I confess, were first
her attraction for me; they are both in the
big grey eyes, which, I said, contemplate
merely, for mere contemplation must needs be
ironical. But I fear you would not have called

her intellectual. Like the great Duchess
Sarah's, her books were men and cards, and
she would talk wittily and with discernment
of her readings of them: of the intrigues,
and passions, and aspirations, and rebuffs of
her acquaintance: her listener pluming himself, belike, with the useless explanations of
philosophy.

And the pivot of her life was sense. She
did not rave, nor, on the other hand, did she
exquisitely philander. Her front was sedate;
but beneath it the old motor of the world was
strong in her, and at its behest she was unscrupulous. Her carriage had the immobility
and polish that society demanded; but her
heart was simple and direct, and knew not to
torture itself with misgivings. But, as I told
you, she was not made for grand passions; it
was bargain for bargain with her; power and
the other good things of life she would not
throw away when address might keep them.
For the rest, selfishness did not exclude kind-
ness, for gratitude is pleasant to hear; her
dependants found her a considerate despot,
her friends an attentive counsellor. I should
like to have known this lady in the flesh; but
the knowledge I have is surer.

MATTER AND FORM

E are suffering from a mental plethora. The statement is made with a full consciousness of the ease of the retort that such a plethora is not obvious in the most of us; and the reply is as easy, that excess is relative to capacity for assimilation. But perhaps it is safer to place the very average person on one side, and to direct such criticism as occurs to an outsider to the immense host, growing out of all proportion to our increase in population, of people in these islands who call themselves, or are called of their acquaintance, intellectual. The habit of these is to snatch with avidity at any utterance possessing the semblance of novelty in its substance—substance is emphatic—at the dinner-table, in the theatre, in the drawing-room, to make a fraction of it their own, and to reproduce it presently with a fine air of thoughtful innovation.

Now, 'to eat or drink,' says Aristotle of the body, 'whatever be your fare, until you be

71

' more than filled, is to exceed the natural
' limit in quantity,' and he goes on to pass a
moral censure on them that thus exceed. One
would apply his proposition to mental gour-
mands, and, omitting the moral censure in the
temporary lack of a determined moral standard,
proceed to mark the consequences : a barren
capping of so-called new theories in conversation and a detrimental confusion of half-ideas
in the rare intervals of thought. These among
others ; but if you be satisfied of the truth of
a dubious doctrine that superficiality is bad,
you may add that consequence also. Sometimes there is a considerable capacity for
assimilation, which in the process of exceeding
demands upon it fails ; most often, however,
the whole mental life of these erring brothers
and sisters is as if a man wholly ignorant of
mechanical science should spend his days in an
engine-room, gazing blankly there at revolving
wheels.

Handbooks, summaries, and the like do
greatly encourage to this habit, and facilitate in
these people a tedious affectation of omniscience
and a most mean avoidance of the commonplace. Intellectual affectation has been seen
before under the sun, and so it is desirable to
distinguish. It is suggested, then, that whereas
the pretty wits of other days sought as a rule
to amuse or render envious their acquaintance

with new conceits of words—new similes, it
might be, or puns—your earnest intellects of
these sadder times seek to astonish you with
new conclusions, depending on new premises,
or a new assemblage thereof.   It may be
thought that a futile contrast is made here of
two types having nothing in common.   In
truth, they are essentially the same ; both are
innocent of real thinking, both possess mediocre
powers of thought, and both seek an easy reputation for thought.   The method it is that is
all the difference ; and with a convenient
crudity, defiant of metaphysics, let us say that
the one studies matter, the other studied form,
in their achievements.

Some advantage, at least, had the latter. A
new phrase is a new phrase, a new form is a
new form.   The idea conveyed may be the
tritest of commonplaces ; but novelty of expression is novelty, and the achievement is
within the reach of many.   Whereas only one
here and there may hope to produce a new
general idea, the rest can only say what has
been said before.   Accordingly, when the
novel idea has been considered a while, it is
found very old ; and the expression of it being
by hypothesis careless, what remains ?   Any
contradiction there may be in this position is
concentrated here for the convenience of the
critical eye.   But the critical eye may be left

to see that between a *soi-disant* new idea, expressed any way and discovered subsequently to be old, and the bright phrasing of a candid commonplace, there is all the difference in the world.

The essence of the question being thus set forth, it seems profitable to reflect on the modes, or some of the modes, in which this craze for new matter is indulged at the expense of form. Carelessness of form is perhaps the most obvious feature in modern manners. That it characterises society, especially in Jeames's acceptance of that term, we are informed *ad nauseam* in exaggerated deliveries by more or less adequately qualified judges. They find its cause in the rush after wealth, and all that ; but may be you would place it more truly in the craze for intellectual novelty. For the many women dowered with fine intellect and great learning whom this country has possessed and possesses we are abundantly thankful. Yet the social function of most women has been, above all things, one of form ; to preserve a quality of gracious consideration for small things—small in the sage's list—to which even the insincere little cordialities and irrational little formalities of the shallowest *mondaine* contribute their part. Be it said that this grace has been often, and is often, conserved more truly by women of fine

intellects than by others.   But in the rage of
the unfit for new ideas all this tends to disap-
pear; and the prospect is somewhat mono-
tonous to view.

The excursions and alarums on the subject
of the ' British Stage,' with which a curious
mind is fairly bewildered nowadays, afford
another and perhaps fortunate instance of the
truth of a proposition which may as yet be
obscure.   One would gladly number himself
among those militant apostles who are desirous
of replacing the clap-trap heroics, stereotyped
pathos, and dull clowning, oppressive to our
spirits these many years, with some attempt at
a drama less damaging to nerves and brains.
But most of them, forgetful of the complexity
of our modern lives and thought, of the subtlety
of the change in our social conventions, and of
the invention of printing, would have it that
the stage should inform us on philosophy, social
and other.   There is a playwright of a fine
dramatic instinct : they hail him a prophet.
Picture to yourself the mental condition of a
person who finds in the doctrine that the sins
of the fathers are visited upon the children a
novel theory.   No doubt such an one has heard
of the Bible and Weismann by this time ; but
he will serve.   The cry is for new ideas.   And
lesser men rush in, and one is weary of
crude presentations of social problems, of self-

conscious and ineffectual philosophising. Is
not a new comedy of manners chiefly to seek ?
Sophocles ! But we live under different con-
ditions from those of the ancient Athenians,
and the mode of our studies does not incite us
to enjoy the motives of such plays as the
Œdipus Rex for two hours after dinner. You
see, specialism is the transitory phase in the
learned, and therefore Nemesis must be
studied in laboratories or bulky products
thereof. A pamphlet drama can only appeal
—to use a convenient and invidious phrase—
to the pit and the gallery. Said the Wise
Youth : ' All wisdom is mournful. 'Tis there-
' fore, coz, that the wise do love the Comic
' Muse. Their own high food would kill them.
' You shall find great poets, rare philosophers,
' night after night on the broad grin before a
' row of yellow lights and mouthing masks.
' Why ? Because all 's dark at home. The
' stage is the pastime of great minds. That 's
' how it comes that the stage is now down.
' An age of rampant little minds, my dear
' Austin !' Surely the play-house should in-
vite us, as Juvenal his friend, to forget un-
faithful wives and ungrateful friends. This it
may by taking our minds from them, or by
presenting them with the noble frivolity of a
Congreve. Let bathos and imbecility be re-
formed away, by all means ; but not to be

replaced by a superficial examination of our peculiar sores.

But the plaint grows tedious, and a multitude of instances may be omitted.   Sincerity is sometimes counted as good as truth, and at least the dread is sincere that in a few years, if this craze for mental novelty persist, we shall have cause to be melancholy.   Then with 'tape' ticking out new ideas in every room, with prophets on every hearth-rug, with mouths that cannot smile and brains that cannot think to any purpose, we shall tremble and turn and endeavour vainly to be changed.

INSOMNIA

O drink and play the night through, and become, with no interval of oblivion, a sober and respectable unit in the morning, had its charms for boyhood. To reconcile yourself to sleeplessness and read or write till they call you to breakfast has a tolerably sustaining air of manly determination and triumph over the brute. But to go to the longed-for bed stupid with sleep, feel sleep coming over you speedily, and never sleep at all—that is the torture of the gods.

Their instrument is that attribute of you the metaphysicians make much of—your power to be outside and observe your sensations, your consciousness of past and future. For as some half-dream, herald, irrelevant, and grotesque, of slumber comes upon your brain, you observe its approach, and are glad, and are wide awake. It comes and withdraws for an hour, and then you are rid of it altogether. You raise yourself on your elbow and reflect. Nerves! Too much work or too much play,

what matter? What signifies your credit or
reproach? Your concern is with this insuper-
able night; you try again to conquer it; but
your made-up dreams are futile, and again
you are thrown back upon realities. Then a
more serious vein is yours; but the paltry
irritation of your nerves unfits your mind from
dwelling on the prime and wholesome facts of
life, and you are not like to face the *nox per-
petua*, and what is irrevocable in your history.
You rather bethink yourself that the world is
treating you scurvily, until your vanity, which
rejects the picture of yourself under anybody's
foot, or your sense of justice, if you prefer it,
leads you to argue on the world's side : you
deserve its treatment of you ; you have had
your money's worth ; there are excuses for
this man's ingratitude, that woman's forgetfulness ; he is not, after all, so unworthy of
your friendship, nor she of your love. You
feel a pressing need of contentment, and even
make little of your friends' follies, their witless
enthusiasms and ludicrous preferences. And
now you deem yourself contented enough for
sleep, which again will have none of you.

You light the gas and open the book you
took to bed from habit. But fatigue has
deprived you of emotional appreciation ; you
have no sympathetic terror as you read De
Quincey's dreams, or, if you go to the other

pole, no delighted chuckle for Jane Austen's irony. The more commonplace matter is, however, your better friend, and you close your eyes and have a brief half-dream of yourself snubbing the colossal snobbery of Emma. Encouraged, you turn out the gas, compose yourself carefully, and are fully conscious once more. . . .

At this stage you fancy for yourself a superiority over the healthy, snoring boors you imagine at rest elsewhere. Then questioning if the unwholesomely abnormal be finer than the common state, you are led to philosophising on the relation of genius to madness, until you feel that a devil in your head has tied a rope round your brain and is pulling steadily. Will your constant sleepless ness end in madness or an early death? You take a dose, but your mind is stronger than that amount of chloral the doctor allows you, and the conviction is despair. But gradually you begin again to entertain dreams, hundreds of them in maddening succession. One moment you are dreaming, the next you are reasoning on the dream's history. The growing light through the curtains serenely reproaches you. At last you sleep for an hour; then healthy humanity is on your nerves again, and you join it with a dazed understanding and dimmed perceptions. Your mother, and your sisters, and your wife, they are people in a dream country, until the gods cease their torture and will you sleep. I pray that the sea or sport may bring it to you, or that time may kill some unacknowledged root of your unquiet. For your sacrifices to the cruel goddess Insomnia are more than a man may well afford.

NATURE'S GREATEST
MISTAKE

BY A VERY YOUNG FRIEND

'THE most uncompromising evolu-
'tionist admits that species have
'been developed and died out.
'They have died because, al-
'though the points which differ-
'entiated them from the preceding species were
'of temporary service, they proved at last in-
'adequate to the needs of the situation. There
'is a product of evolution which has been for
'centuries and centuries of incalculable ser-
'vice to its possessors, but has become, here
'and now, an hindrance and a curse. There-
'fore must it die, though none may pen its
'epitaph. For I refer to the later development
'of the human intellect.

'It is like enough that you may be uncon-
'vinced by the bare assertion, may even count
'the writer of it among them that deal in
'paradox. I am fain to answer merely: "My

' " brother, my poor brothers, it is thus." But
' having so far departed from my service to that
' great religion of inaction which offers the only
' possible remedy—and a very uncertain—of the
' dissolution as to speak of it at all, I will bend
' my baser nature, arguing and illustrating.
' When men were not men, and were fighting
' for their Helens with their teeth, the begin-
' nings of the quality which was to make them
' men, or something like men, in the fulness of
' time, gave him in whom it coyly sprouted life
' over his fellows. He hardened the end of a
' stick. So, mainly in this direction did intellect
' develop, until in the Mother Age (if that be
' still a scientific hypothesis) it was used for
' milking. There were hosts and huts. Then
' come the singer and the sculptor and the
· philosopher, and the beginning of our tale.

'I propose to show that the more complex
' and rarer qualities of intellect are a curse
' to their possessors, and must die out. It
' might, perhaps, be shown that the less com-
' plex, with their Midases and industrial crises,
' are not good. When these are unfit, however,
' they have their punishment; submersion by
' barbarians, or a revolution. But they are
' perhaps seldom bad in my sense, as bringing
' woe on their possessors. Your prosperous
' fellow likes himself hugely, as a rule. Or if
' he be anæmic and nervous, those nearest him

' are happy under the sun in their way; whereas
' nothing is more certain than that the people
' about the children of light are irritated by
' their presence. No: it is the finer intellect,
' with its sense of shades, its perception of
' subtle misunderstandings, its hopelessness,
' which is miserable all the days of its life.

 ' They say the countrymen of Plato were a
' happy folk. People say this who have read
' Æschylus and Sophocles—read the *Antigone*—
' and Aristophanes, that mine of witty and joy-
' less mirth. Men are not sad because they can
' love a sad play. But the tone of these plays,
' these choruses, seems surely to show that the
' Greek mind perceived well enough the tragic
' element in our little farce. And as surely as
' we approach in temper the level of the think-
' ing Athenian we perceive this tragic element
' the more clearly; and when we have congratu-
' lated ourselves that at last we can greet the
' creeds and successes and failures of our fellows
' and of ourselves with a patient smile, we are
' near the sorrow that is too bitter for tears.
' Congreve was an Athenian of a wit as joyless
' as Aristophanes. And so the Greeks died of
' their intellect; for Greeks nowadays are on
' the Stock Exchange. The cure they—some of
' them—found was not to think so much: who
' would not be Anacreon, and drink more in his
' age than the young men?

'With ourselves, we can come to more de-
' tailed illustration. It is on all sides, for on all
' sides are perceptions and powers of reason
' which know themselves blunted and wasted
' amid stupid obstacles and vulgar insipidities.
' Some of them are yet imbued with the Puritan
' superstition that "duty" is worth all else, and
' so are moderately happy. And the others?
' This one locks up his better intellect until it
' dies of disuse. That one cuts off its finer edges,
' and tricks it out, and brings it—the gods pity
' him !—into the market-place that he may eat
' a piece of bread. Observing these two, we see
' that to both their intellectual development is
' an hindrance to happiness, and consequently a
' check in the race of life. They tend, there-
' fore, to die off, and die they will. And, lastly,
' there is one whose intellect is backed up by
' ancestral acres or brewing : what of him ? He
' may avoid the blatant and the mean when the
' others may not ; he may select in comparative
' peace ; he may, far more than the others,
' appreciate the here and now. Grant him not
' to have married a dolt at twenty, and not to
' have any marked physical infirmity. But he
' is yet a unit. He has social instincts, and if
' he lives in the desert their dissatisfaction will
' render him wretched. If he goes into the
' world, whoever be his friends and his "friends,"
' his subtle perceptions and complex imaginings

' will be jarred always. This may seem to be
' ironical, but it is very true, and not the least
' sad of human wastings. He will assuredly be
' misunderstood, assuredly involved in all the
' current make-beliefs and mild hypocrisies
' necessary to an imperfect civilisation; and
' some will take these in him seriously. His
' body, moreover, healthy by hypothesis, has
' needs whose crushing and whose satisfaction
' alike, among a hypocritical people, will prob-
' ably blur what is best in him. He, too, is the
' worse for his best.

' "But," you say, "these three types have
' "always existed. In every age there are some
' "a little in advance of their generation; in
' "every succeeding age there are others." Yes,
' but their subject-matter was different. The
' finer intellects of our day, or most of them, no
' longer wish to fight with superstitions; they
' are only sorry they do not share them. Or to
' rail against prejudices: they cherish such as
' they have left to them. Or to preach a new
' religion: their religion, if they have one, is
' personal to themselves. We all have come to
' know that, for "all our weeping, waking, and
' "sleeping, death comes to reaping, and takes
' "away." But they are convinced, emotionally
' as well as intellectually, that this is all their
' personal life. And of what use to tell me that
' I shall be absorbed into the Universal Mind

'and live for ever?   I want *my* mind, with its
'individual cranks and its personal affections
'and hatreds.   Logically I should gather roses?
'But that is not natural to the man convinced,
'emotionally, that the flood is coming over the
'next field.'

Thus a young friend in a time of fog and
trouble: I laughed with him partly, but also
at him, for I thought he meant one or two of
his remarks.

CRUELTY

YES: no doubt it is a dreadful re-flection that the Sunday school and the penny press have not eradicated all the primitive in-stincts. But, you see, delight in others' suffering is a very old delight indeed: older than most of the hills. To say nothing of lionesses and so on, cruelty was developed in the first men who fought. From an ex-pression of anger it passed into a settled love of suffering for its own sake. Surely one may dogmatise on these things? But if you need an alternative dogma, take it that cruelty may be analysed into love of power. To inflict pain at will is the easiest and most obvious mode of showing power; a less obvious way is the way of kindnesses. Not infrequently you may see both expressions of power in the same person. But the thought grows sad, as is all analysis.

Penny press and Sunday school are impotent to eradicate primitive instincts. But they may alter the outward and visible signs. They and their like have brought it about that the most cruel by nature do not bait badgers; with mouths full of pious and enlightened purposes, they 'crucify hearts, not hands.' A more refined and civilised occupation, surely, but hardly less cruel? You need not to occupy your attention with wife-beaters and child-torturers. There is much of this old cruelty, no doubt, among us—perhaps more than is dreamed of. But as a rule it is not pure cruelty, being adulterated with anger, revenge, jealousy, and the like. And it is not interesting to you, unless you be of those shallow optimists who think to pull down bad passions like a row of condemned cottages. There is a latter-day cruelty, not of the flesh, which is pure enjoyment of others' suffering. It goes under many names : curiosity, justice, even its old alias religion : so that those fair forms have sometimes blood on their skirts. But as in the middle ages Nature, smarting from the ineffectual fork, impelled holy men to write hymns to their Virgin which knights sang of their light-o'-loves, so now may you discover, while words of morality or prudence or piety are in your ears, and irreproachable ugliness of garments is before your eyes, the feelings of your ancestors. Most often this passion has a fair beginning. 'He will not,' said one pedagogue of another, 'entertain mercy while there

' is room for justice'; and this justice is not seldom the excuse. Justice is for public dealing, for 'business,' laws, what you will; be a just merchant, a just judge, a just legislator, and guard yourself so against any taint of sentiment; but if you be a just friend or a just lover, you are bloodless—or cruel! I find in you a tendency to assert this justice too often and too loudly. For, mark you, it is only when your friend or your mistress may be hurt by justice that your attention is drawn to it. So with our dear Coquette. She is young and her little cruelties are charming: no man, I grant you, worth his salt but loves them, and no man (not an ill-bred prig) who thinks they need forgiveness. But in ten years' time she will be young no more, when should we still find her course attended by wasted boys and weeping mothers, our dear Coquette will be interesting from our present point of view. The more so, in that she shows herself but a primitive woman, who is waiting for the primitive man to bully her. Him she will love well enough, and her court must learn that domination or indifference—not submission and long service—is the way to the primitive woman's heart. Dear Lady Coquette! her joy in inflicting pain is cruelty, but the joy she will take in suffering is the world's recompense. I, for my part, have no quarrel with her.

And need one quarrel with the tribe who go about with God knows what professions to hoot and howl at some detected sinner? Their ancestors threw eggs and mud at the man in the stocks, wherein themselves should stand in due season. Cruelty is too fine a word for their quality. But it is fitted most aptly to some of those who crowd to the courts of justice. God forbid that I should write of gladiatorial shows and arenas and down-turned thumbs. The thing has been used up, and is unclean. But if you look very carefully round you will find some there who come not to gaze upon celebrity or to listen to forensic eloquence, but because they are cruel, and descend to this wretched substitute for bull- and bear-baiting.

These few indications of how a primitive passion will persist might be multiplied many times. Go with them in your mind, and analyse the motives at work in the little dramas of your circle. If you do so thoughtfully and painfully enough, you will end as desperate a fool as I am. I would not, however, have you raise your hands to heaven. Cruelty is a part of human economy that may not be spared. In fine, it is a defect of many admirable qualities, and so I take my leave of it.

THE CURSE OF CLEVERNESS

THE shallow little intellect, radiating with acute little glances, and possessed altogether by the fallacies of strict logic, is not a curse to itself. Rather, it enjoys itself amid the tributes of the pachydermatous. Secure in the limits of its perception, it is proof against the sarcasms of its betters. But O the relentless irritation and ineffable weariness of it to you and me! If we go up into the heights of science, it is there; if we descend to the uttermost depths of the penny press, it is there also. It has read a little handbook, and assimilated partly a little idea; and it is prepared to crush the great gods because their great ideas do not include the little idea which is to be found in the little handbook.

You may have blessed yourself once and again that you are hearing a man who has something to say. He has a thought to share. It must be unprepared and therefore dim in a way, and in the imperfection of divine English

the words may be inaccurate. But you see
the drift; he is suggesting more than he can
say, and the heaven of heavens is coming into
view, when in steps perky Impertinence and
with tin-tacks of logic nails him to the plane
where two and two make four, and A is either
B or not-B. He may have had all the pathos
of an old intriguer, all the wisdom of a young
lover; but A is either B or not-B, and so the
subject dropped. And Cleverness, when he is
gone, hints that paradoxes are tedious, and,
confessing a preference for intellectual conversation, starts you on the scheme for national
insurance. And you long for the society of an
idiot.

Or you may have seen a woman in a million
wasting her preciousness on a clever young
man. Without the courage to comprehend,
or the wit to worship, he sits smiling ever
complacently, and stops the essence of a life's
pitiful successes or fruitful failures with some
dictum, born dead and damned, about the
progress of the species. She had been tried
by fire, but, you see, she had not read his
little handbook. You need make no apology
for arrogance in speaking thus of attorney's
brains misapplied. Whatever we may think,
we do not say that we have broader minds and
keener perception. But we know our place,
and the fact that other men have made it

possible for us to exceed our betters in knowledge has not taken away from us all capacity
for admiration.   A stupid acquiescence in an
older judgment (that Addison is a god, for
instance) is one thing; the power to perceive
there is one Sir Walter is another thing.   There
is an autograph of the First Charles in the
British Museum.   ' If a man being freed of
' superstition, grow to be profane,' asks he,
' what hath he gotten ? '

In literature you may always take of the
best (for you); in life but seldom.   What
then ?   There is a river where one may free
himself from cleverness, may wash and be
clean.   It is called the Stream of Stupidity ;
and, floating down it in restful content, you
leave Cleverness gibbering on the bank.   Many
a weary man has known the restfulness of
languid conversation with a thoroughly stupid
person.   *He* does not perceive that you use
his mind as a cushioned chair.   *She* does not
resent that, while you seem to hear her comments on life, you are nursing memories.   The
Stream of Stupidity is also the River of Dreams.
There is yet another reason for its place among
the rarest gifts of Heaven.   The union of a fine
intellect with a great nature may be rare ; that
of a clever little intellect with a good nature
is harder to find ; but a kindly and tolerant
heart is often wedded to—no intellect at all.

And among our acquaintances we sometimes have need of friends.

A fine intellect is a glorious thing ; stupidity is its proper and necessary balance ; but cleverness that comes between, and fills our lives with irritation and dulness—out upon it !

THE ETERNAL SUBJECT

FOR so long time as men shall express themselves in words, they must need to write largely of what is at least the half of their lives. Indeed, if you analyse enough you will find that in civilised man 'love,' as they call it, is directly or indirectly the central motive of far more than the half of his comedies and tragedies. The word, of course, stands for the genus, and the species is seldom indicated as clearly as it might be. 'Love' stands for mere desire, and sometimes for strong affection, and usually for a combination—in varying proportions—of the two. Anacreon sang the love that is desire and appreciation of beauty, and Sappho the love that is desire excited to mania; Horace the love that is desire and mild affection, and Catallus love in all its phases—brute desire and affectionate desire and desire that goes hand in hand with hate. Let us limit our view and keep to the English novelist. Or rather, let us be refreshed with a glance at

our great ones, and then turn to the little ones;
for it is difficult to share another's gladness,
but all will lend ear to a complaint themselves
have surely felt.

The love which comes upon two virginal
hearts at once, which is pure at its foundation
and builds no superstructure of make-believe
and false sentiment on desire—this love is told
as none else has told it in *Richard Feverel*. Of
the approach of two natures without a sexual
past, without regrets, without comparisons,
while Mother Nature showed how goodly and
wholesome a thing this natural impulse un-
defiled by sophistry may be, and how fair to
watch are its beginnings of emotion—of this
phase there is hardly such an epic in prose
elsewhere. One remembers other phases.
Fielding has given us most of them in his
robust instinct, Richardson has displayed the
sentimental aspect, and Sterne has smiled on
the easy ardour of my Uncle Toby for the
Widow Wadman. Mr. Arthur Pendennis
illustrates several in his own worthy person;
and when Henry Esmond, cheated of Beatrix,
fell back on the object of his boyish worship,
even Trix's mother, and married her, there
was written one of the boldest and most
excellent things in fiction. But an enumera-
tion would be impertinent. . . . All the phases
are illustrated by our greater novelists, or all

save one or two. To come to our complaint
of the smaller ones and to take them in the
lump. The plaint is not that they write of
love, which, as was said, is half of life, and
instead thereof one would not have them trace
the details of the hero's financial operations,
or concern themselves with the minutiæ of
engines and dynamos. The grievance is, that
their loves are always the loves of little-hearted
virgins and nice young men. Even in the
greater masters you find a general tendency
to place two young persons in the limelight,
so that the thing is sometimes tedious. Of
such love as was Richard Feverel's and Lucy's,
no reader may complain; but, frankly, the
young person whose love is always being
sickled o'er with this or that fantasy or
mishap is wearisome. The young woman
for this reason. Surely we know that most
often she can hardly feel an intensity
of passion before marriage, and therefore
her suspicions and questionings and self-
deceptions are not often of constraining
interest. We wax weary of the damsel who
discards her lover for groundless jealousy, of
the school-girl who is for reclaiming the repentant rake (so he said), of her who proclaims
her zeal to be for the cause and not the man.
Our little novelists, being mostly women, treat
of these things with tolerable accuracy; but

the things are in themselves barren. And the young male is ineffably wearisome, because, our little novelists being mostly women, he figures in their pages as either prig or cad. The woman who can draw an amiable virile man in his time of passion is a jewel indeed. Even Charlotte Brontë, she who could make her plain, insignificant little governesses absolutely adorable, of how many male lovers has she given the impression of manliness and humanity, if you except M. Paul? And one speaks of novelists with other powers than hers.

There is a minor point worth noting. Granting the interest of the bloodless philandering of young people, one finds that in defiance of experience and of the best proverb on the subject their loves are almost always mutual. This either postulates that the emotions of variously conditioned people always develop at an equal speed, which is absurd, or ignores the sad fact that neither with man nor with woman does the sight of passion in another stimulate a return, for there is nothing to be won, and the return is often the deception of self or of others. Mutual, contemporaneous devotion is the gift given to the very few: yet our little novelists attest it the privilege of all but villains. But that incessant procession of inane young persons from the absurd love at first sight to the lawful altar is what grieves the wise. For they tell us that middle-aged passion is a sterner and more fruitful thing than the rambling inclination of mistaken school-girls. Of course our little novelists have no claim to rank as artists; they do not try to express their best, but merely to supply a demand. All the more reason they should list now and then to the demand of the wise. For though the wise read few new novels, yet when they are catholic they like a touch of modernity in their reading; and when, seeking it, they find but the ancient young person, they are troubled. Or suppose our little novelists did endeavour after art. It is true that the first purpose of a work of art is not to set one thinking; but an art whose concern is with the qualities of human beings must be jejune if it raise no secondary question of the philosophy of sex. The suggestions of little novelists are not likely to be valuable; in point of art they must of necessity be slipshod and futile. But if their love stories bore some relation to their knowledge of life—even to theirs—they would be none the less profitable and a deal less annoying to read.

A MODERN VERSION

THE Youth came from Balliol to the cross-ways, where stood a man and a woman. The man was tall, and of a firm jaw and clear eyes; straight was he and square-shouldered, but to the youth there seemed a clumsiness in his carriage and a lack of intelligence in the shape of his forehead. The woman was plump and comely and easy of bearing; she showed her white teeth to the youth as she would smile, but the look in her eyes was anxious.

And the man said: 'O youth, we are friends; 'I am called Duty.'

And the youth replied: 'You are indeed 'called Duty by many; but your right to the 'name is at best occasional, and analysis may 'show it a convention. I know you well, and 'you are merely Work.'

To the woman he said: 'It is courtesy to 'call you Pleasure. Yet have you no monopoly 'of the title, which is sometimes to be borne

101

' by Work. Often you are grievous and a very
' millstone. Everything is relative, and this
' matter is one of inherited impulses and
' acquired habits. Let me therefore state the
' personal equation, that your arguments may
' be simplified. I have acquired no habit of
' liking Work (frankness is the mode to-day),
' and my heritage impels me to enjoy you,
' who are as yet Pleasure in truth to me, as
' long as I may.'

' Come, then,' quoth she, ' and enjoy.'

' Nay, come with me,' quoth the man, ' and
' I will lead you to Heaven.'

' Alas! good man,' said the youth, ' the time
' is gone by for such an argument. You would
' say you mean something else than the tales
' I was told as a boy, but the catch-words of
' philosophy do not make a hypothesis philo-
' sophical. Moreover, the object is grossly
' utilitarian—merely my own enjoyment of the
' hereafter, and Pleasure will give it me now.
' Tell me something less selfish.'

' The greatest good of the greatest number,'
said the man.

' You make brave strides, but are yet behind
' the times. Bentham's system was not a Pig-
' philosophy, as said Carlyle, and its utilitarian-
' ism (unlike your heavenly theory's) is un-
' selfish. But—pardon my popular erudition—
' Green has shown it inadequate in theory,

' and I defy you to prove that in practice my
' following you would promote the end you
' give me.'

 ' Well, then, the satisfaction of your friends.'

 ' Ah ! that,' said the youth, ' is more reason-
' able and human. But you surely wrong them,
' if you think an irksome servitude of me to
' you would satisfy them. Their chief wish for
' me, I am assured, is my own satisfaction, and
' I must be left to judge of that ; if their
' theories are unreasonable, it is my business
' as a friend to ignore them.'

Then the man frowned, and said : ' A truce
' to your quibbles. There are very many who
' must follow me or starve, and are you not
' ashamed——— '

 ' Not in the least degree,' rejoined the youth.
' I am a convinced Socialist, and the doctrine of
' Socialism is that every one of us should work.'
The woman laughed, and tapped the ground im-
patiently with her foot. ' But it has been shown,
' time and again, that the practice of Socialism
' by isolated individuals does no good to the
' unjustly worked, but rather benefits the un-
' justly idle, if the community practises it
' not. The chief advantage of our present
' monstrous polity is in a variety of types ;
' now England is a dull country to-day, and
' most of us care too little for this lady.
' Therefore shall I best mitigate the condi-

' tion of my fellows by being her servant.
' No, my friend that would be, return you
' to selfish arguments.'

'Ambition,' murmured the other—' Premier
' . . . the woolsack.'

' Vulgarity !' returned the youth in disdain :
' these tempt me not. What ? To toil like a
' slave for years and years, toil far more griev-
' ously than any in that blessed state of Social-
' ism I hope will arrive, to the doubtful end
' that I be applauded by a despicable rabble,
' and be used by a mob of place-hunters ?
' Why, this,' and he took the woman's hand
and kissed it, ' is no more gross an end than
' that, and is at least substantial. But I am
' glad you did not call it an unselfish end, and
' speak of "serving my country." '

' Art,' said the man, ' the best expression of
' yourself in words, or in sounds, or in lines and
' colours.'

' You touch me more nearly,' said the other ;
' but life is more than art, and there are other
' media of expression than colours and sounds
' and words. Yet is the aim at least likely to
' be free from vulgar recognition. Now, listen,'
he said, ' listen, both of you. You have been
' following this cross-ways business for thou-
' sands of years, and must have learned by
' experience that your immemorial quarrel is
' superfluous in great measure. In so far as it is

'wholly irreconcileable, it is the remnant of an
'ascetic superstition that the world is weary
'of. It is possible for such as I am to go with
· both of you. The end of life is life, and the
'fullest life is the life most complex, in which
'every faculty is duly exercised. In the best
'equilibrium of existence a man goes with you
'by turns, or rather with both at once. But
'I grant you there is something calculating,
'and therefore possibly unamiable, in this pro-
'cedure, and it is yet an effect of a state of
'transition that we admire an whole-hearted
'self-abandonment. Possibly some play on the
'nerves, some experience of life, is to be gained
'in this way. Therefore I shall act thus: I shall
'abandon myself wholly to you, Pleasure, while
'youth is with me. *Donec virenti* . . . it is
'a very old tale. But, Work, I shall some day
'perhaps ask your company, and perchance
'with your assistance (for without it man is
'mostly helpless) achieve something of that
'last ambition you named to me. Does it
'content you ?'

The man said it contented him not. 'And
'I have one other argument, and that is she.'

And the youth was aware of a second woman,
whose qualities you can best imagine for yourself. It is enough to say that to the youth she
seemed a thing divine. Pleasure was pretty,
but Happiness (so the youth named her) was

beautiful, and the youth called her beauty
spiritual. Pleasure was graceful, but Happiness was distinguished and a queen. And the
youth knelt and worshipped her.

She said : ' I forbid you to go with Pleasure ;
' go you with Duty, and perchance you may
' attain unto me.'

And the youth said : ' Will you not pro-
' mise ? '

And she : ' Your journey with Duty will be
' long, and many things may happen to me
' before its end. Live in hope,' she said, and
was gone, and the youth rose up and looked
foolishly.

' It is a selfish object after all,' he sighed, and
the woman sneered and said : ' Yes, indeed.
' And she and I are sisters, after all.'

' Not so,' said the youth ; ' your lineage is
' ancient, and you have not mended the appear-
' ance of your first ancestress. She comes from
' the same stock, but the generations have
' added qualities you have not. There is desire
' and there is love, which is desire and affec-
' tion and esteem.'

The woman laughed, and said : ' Go your
' ways, Youth, and follow this will-o'-the-wisp.
' But know that if Happiness cheat you,
' and you come back to me in later life, you
' will come not as a friend, as you may now,
' but as a thrall for ever. I shall drive you

' before me, and when you faint I shall strike
' you with a whip.'

So the woman left them, and the man and the youth set forth together.

But whether he found Happiness was Congreve's woman, 'the reflection of Heaven in a pond; and he that leaps at her is sunk,' and so returned to Pleasure and her whip, or Happiness rejoined him and the man (whom he would then call Duty) and made their road pleasant, . . . it is very much a toss-up.

THE PATH OF REJECTION

WE begin by accepting most things, and, if the discipline of our minds have been of a certain order, we end by rejecting nearly all. This commonplace has many illustrations, and on it doubtless many a sage and sad reflection has been uttered. One or two bright ones might be added to complete the truth; for if we have outworn our loves, yet our loves they have been, and we may say there is a pride of intellect not altogether futile in the ultimate passage to indifference: which pride is pleasant. For the worthless indifference and for the pretentious dislike are allowed you; contempt for modest lack of brains or learning is another thing— the mere snobbery of intellect or learning. Remembering this, you may go on your path of rejection blameless, and reach the goal with what appetite you may. After all, it will go hard but that some few of the world's artists shall content you to the end of your days.

This of the things in the field of taste and

judgment less dependent on the circulation of
the blood.   Our tiring of the rest means
physical weakness, of course, and so in all the
warmth of our acceptance is according to our
temperament: some will be enthusiastic over
that which leaves others, who have, emotion
apart, a like appreciation, unperturbed.   Our
taste and judgment may become more and
more exquisite, while our vitality becomes less
and less abundant, and ourselves critical and
merely *blasé* at the same time.   *Nil admirari*,
or something like that, is an attribute of both
states.

When we reject persons, it is most often
for good and all.   The relations who loomed
large in our childhood, only because they had
the (now very disputable) advantage of matu-
rity; the sham *roués* who imposed on our
adolescence with their brag of common dis-
sipation; the women who flattered our early
manhood with hopes of comprehension: they
are all gone, and their place on our horizon
knoweth them no more.   We may—but I
would hope it was otherwise—have been be-
guiled by the platitudes of progress in our
conceit of emancipation; or by the worship
of the bloodless, merely a reaction from the
necessary brute within us; or by the cult of
cleverness, which was our revolt against the
healthy stupidity around us.   They are all gone

for ever.   In books, too, some sorts of jocosity
and pathos please us no more.

But with most things there is rejection, and
after a space acceptance on other terms.
Dogmas learned early are despised and again
valued—not as dogmas but—as half-true criticism of life.   We are shut out of fairyland,
again, for a while, and are fain to re-enter
later on : we make but clumsy figures there, it
may be, and are no longer full citizens, but as
visitors we are humble and grateful enough.
The scenes that seemed—ah ! hundreds of
years ago—to embody life and gaiety have
once more, after a period of contempt for the
monotonies of folly, some attraction of humanity.   And Horace (say), despised for a time,
while our mighty philosophy seemed to lay
bare his shallows, draws us back by his sureness,
and we attain at length to a sense of his perfection.   And so forth; and the refusal of
some kinds of the worse is a condition of the
acceptance of the better.   Do not, therefore,
ask me to pity you unless your case be in this
wise.   You may have created, and you may have
to reject much of your own.   How, then, have
you hated those earlier inanities which are all
the run of your friends care for !   Sometimes
you may be at fault: yours may be the case of
comfortable middle-age frowning on the less
trammelled and worthier commissions of the

hot season. I fear, though, that as a rule your condemnation of those poems and stories is just enough. But you may desire still to create, and your faculty for it may lag behind the improvement of your judgment. Then I am sorry in truth, for you come to a deadlock. As t' other afternoon you took the occasion of solitude, and settled down to a work of genius : everything was still, the air persuaded you softly, the sky smiled approval. But, alas o' day, the genius was all critical. Poetical rhapsody, cynical analysis, observant philo- sophy—never a one would serve you. This was crude, that ancient, the other superficial. In the end your paper was innocent. And how many of these pages would you have passed that afternoon ?

Printed by T. and A. CONSTABLE, Printers to Her Majesty, at the Edinburgh University Press.

Lightning Source UK Ltd.
Milton Keynes UK
UKHW020955150421
382040UK00006B/546